CHUCK BERRY

CHUCK BERRY

MR. ROCK N' ROLL BY

KRISTA REESE

Proteus Books
London and New York

PROTEUS BOOKS is an imprint of
The Proteus Publishing Group.

United States
PROTEUS PUBLISHING CO., INC.
733 Third Avenue
New York, NY 10017

distributed by
THE SCRIBNER BOOK COMPANIES, INC.
597 Fifth Avenue
New York, NY 10017

PROTEUS (PUBLISHING) LTD
Bremar House
Sale Place
London W2 1PT

ISBN 086276 018 6 (paperback)
086276 041 0 (hardback)

First published in UK 1982
First published in US 1982

Art Direction: Rocking Russian

Design: Baillie Walsh

Typeset by TJB Photosetting Ltd., South Witham, Lincolnshire

Photo Credits: Lynn Goldsmith; National Film Archive/Stills Library; Jill Furmanovsky; UPI; Rex Features; Joe Simnowski; Marcia Resnick; Syndication International; Malcolm Jones.

Printed by Printer Industria Grafica sa, Barcelona, Spain
D.L.B. 30586-1982.

CONTENTS

True, he was not the sole influence that brought about the revolution, but all the environment, heredity and selective memory that made Chuck Berry a street-walking, jive-talking rhythm and blues upstart somehow crystallized into a figure who would be singled out time and again as the originator of rock & roll. The familiar *chunkita-chunkita-chunkita* riff, regular as a washing machine on a back porch, coupled with sassy, libidinous lyrics is the Chuck Berry signature tune. And after it had bounced around the Rockies and Smokies, it ricocheted across the Atlantic, landing intact in England's port cities. Like the people in the States who acclaimed him and his contemporaries, Little Richard, Jerry Lee Lewis and Elvis Presley, the audience in England was not the lunatic fringe but, well *regional*, working class and young.

Among those listening were John Lennon, Paul McCartney, Mick Jagger, Keith Richards, and scores of others who moulded the sound into their own likeness and brought it back across the sea in a second revolutionary wave.

As important as these later repercussions was the immediate impact on those who heard it. After long nights of scanning the airwaves looking for something new, already primed on R & B, the sound was a sudden awakening, a baptism in ice-cold water. In the throes of adolescent hormonal changes, they would make it an ultra-dramatic, life-or-death obsession. Like newly converted zealots, they spread the good news. Eventually this raunchy incubation became half-respectable, and saw printed criticism. About Berry in particular, writers have said: "the epitome of rock & roll" (Robert Christgau), "emphatically encapsulates the lowdown power of rock & roll" (Jay Cocks), "the creator of rock & roll" (Dave Gelly). Almost everyone in rock today owes something to Berry, whether it is his or her guitar virtuosity, stage showmanship, or precision of lyrics and delivery.

Put Berry in the context of the 50s and he becomes an even more incredible phenomenon. Now the subject of sitcoms, toys and theme parties, the era has become, for some, a Golden Age, glowing with the radiance only nostalgia can give. Maybe some of it is true. It seems easy to believe "kids were happier then" and it was a time of unprecedented economic prosperity. But still, a quick browse through *Life*, *The Saturday Evening Post* or the *Manchester Guardian* tells the whole less palatable truth: it was a white-bread-and-mayonnaise, menopausal sort of existence; gray clothes, gray politics, gray culture. Some have called the sexuality of the time "innocent" or "naive" but Puritans raged unchecked, treading as heavily as they had in 1600 New England. Their greatest fear: Someone, somewhere, might be having a good time.

And, of course, somebody was.

There were rumblings underneath — far below the cellophane smoothness of Pat Boone — singers of the "separate but equal" so-called "race and hot jazz" charts kept popping up, at times threatening to puncture the air-

tight seal the crooners then held on the market. The major labels managed to keep the lid on by having Boone and others cover some R & B hits. It was as if an entire generation had suffered shell shock in World War II and could endure nothing more strenuous than an evening dose of Perry Como.

The first assault came from Bill Haley, which was bad enough, but when Berry's "Maybellene" hit the air straight from Alan Freed's rock & roll party on radio station WINS, all hell broke loose. *This* guy had a souped-up V-8 Ford! He cruised! And the stage show at the Paramount smashed the idyll to bits — this was not warmed-over cowboys swaying with their six strings. This one wrote his own songs. This guy had a scarlet, electric Gibson that he played the shit out of while performing acrobatic feats! This was no plump greaser, but a sinewy, athletic, jumping, living, breathing, sexy (hushed tones of awe and fear) *Nee-gro.*

Not a lot has changed in his performance since those days, except maybe a lessening of the fear and awe, and perhaps the things that happened along the way made the man offstage tougher and harder. Tales of his backstage bad temper and moodiness have become legendary, as well as his shrewd, all-business demeanor. The songs themselves are a lot alike, a variation on a basic theme, but it is a theme that continues to stand up to steadily tougher audiences.

It is impossible to imagine what the last 25 years would have been like without him.

You have to remember that in those days it was not *okay to be a teenager. Being a teenager was wrong.*

No, I couldn't get anyone to go with me to the Paramount. I guess they were too busy listening to Perry Como.

The thing you had to have was a wallet so full of pictures you couldn't close it. Pictures of all your friends, people you didn't know, movie stars, James Dean ... you had to have a leather jacket, and your collar and sleeves turned up, a garrison belt ... Nestle used to make these gold and silver sprays. We used to spray that on our hair before we went out. We used to wear these $3.98 slingbacks. You had to get the kind – they were called low-cut slingbacks. You had to get the kind that came down far enough to show the cracks between your toes. Those were really tough.

What was it like to be in high school in the '50s? For me it was really dull ... Mother was Baptist and we weren't allowed to dance. To her, dancing was just a prelude to sexual frenzy. I remember once I went to a church *dance, and I came home and was so excited. 'Mother! They were all Baptist kids and we danced and it was fun!' She said, 'Well, that's fine. But I don't know why you enjoyed it.'*

Yeah, I remember the first record player I ever had. I was probably 5 or 6 and it was one of those that looked like a little suitcase. You opened it to play and it had the speaker inside. I had these red and yellow vinyl Roy Rogers and Dale Evans 45's my parents had given me, and I would wear these red cowboy boots when I played them. Later on the record player got a bad short in it and you'd have to be really brave to play it. Once I made my little brother change the record. I didn't know it, but he had peed in his pants and was badly shocked. Just started screaming. He was OK, though.

I had a friend who used to sit down and listen to the music ... mystically. *He was sure that the songs held a kind of mystical meaning, and if he listened close enough, he'd find out what it was like to be an adult.*

No, no, I never got any of that from my parents. Even then, New York was hip. Maybe in the Midwest or something, but not here. They were glad I went (to the Paramount) – got me out of their hair for awhile. My childhood was not so good. My parents were getting a divorce ... I think really the music then was one of the few things that kept me going.

EL COME BA K

It all really frightened me. I disliked Elvis and all that intensely . . . I was growing up in Ohio and we heard Lowell Thomas on the news at night; that was all . . . Now that I think of it, I didn't like Frank Sinatra when he came out either. But I really hated Elvis. Later, of course, I changed my mind and liked them. But then it was so different . . .

"Good afternoon, Mercury Records."
"I was wondering if I could speak to someone there who handled publicity for **Chuck Berry**.*"*
"Hmmm . . . Chuck Berry. Would that be classical?"

Oh yes, I'm a great fan. I have a wonderful bootleg of demos and unreleased versions at home. One of the cuts has Otis Spann on it. Did you see him on Tom Snyder? he was just great – dignified and wild at the same time. This middle-aged man sighs. 'Chuck Berry's the man I'd most like to be when I grow up.'

Fall 1981: Madison Square Garden, filled to the rafters with doo-wop fans and 50s afficianados. They seem perfectly willing to coronate the Drifters, and Lou Christie makes lightning strike again. Leslie Gore brings the house down with "You Don't Own Me." But when Chuck Berry takes the stage, this well-behaved group comes unhinged, standing on chairs and howling at the moon. A string of fans are actually skipping through the aisles, hands held, red-rover style.

Culver City, California, 1956: For the making of one of many rock movies that year, Berry appears in a baggy white suit singing with a combo to a total of three white kids in a chocolate shop. The kids sip their sodas and bob their heads, one blond ponytail flipping side to side.

September 1981: The Ritz, New York's snazzy nightclub, showcasing top bands. Instructor Berry lectures the bouncing audience, many of whom are several years younger than Maybellene, in the theories of reelin' and rockin', and they recite on cue.

Come back tomorrow. We'll play more Chuck. We'll have fun. (Keith Richards to an interviewer, 1979)

From the time he walked into the Chess brothers offices on a May day in 1955 with a tape he'd made on a mono recorder, the texture of popular music was forever changed.

1926, and the very air was charged with magical elements. Voices travelled by wire, heroes flew, pictures moved and spoke. But the country was far from stricken with awe at this alchemy. Maybe another environment would have fostered a stern dedication to implementing these inventions in practical ways. But since Scott Joplin, life itself had taken on the jumping, speedy quality of a nickelodeon show.

It was called the Jazz Age, and if old movies and F. Scott Fitzgerald novels are any indication of the climate, the people revelled in all of it and accelerated their lives to match technology's frenzied pace. In the midst of post-war prosperity, there were the beginnings of a new pop culture, complete with clothes (short skirts, no bras, lots of bangles for girls; a straw-hat, raccoon-coat collegiate look for boys), loose morals, slang, and of course, music.

The nation seemed hell-bent on having a good time celebrating its own wondrous induction into the modern world. Enormous technological leaps had been achieved in an almost terrifyingly short time, and there was a frantic urge to push farther and faster. The turn-of-the-century invention of the microphone was one such revolution although Rudy Vallee (one of the first to make girls swoon) still used his megaphone. (He liked the sound.) "Ain't She Sweet" ('27) and "Baby Face" ('26) were top numbers. The family Victrola became a standard item; they were so durable that many were still around the house, trying out

Bill Haley in the 50s. Radio would become an indispensable fixture in the 30s. And just a year after Berry's birth Les Paul attached a ceramic pickup to his acoustic guitar: the electric guitar was invented.

F. Scott Fitzgerald's novels embody this convulsive era of change best, but to most middle-class families, life was not at all like Fitzgerald's partied-out wastrels in *This Side of Paradise*. It was a lot more like Sherwood Anderson's bleached-out inhabitants of *Winesburg, Ohio*. For a black family, it was far worse. Contrasting all those great leaps forward, like the first heavier-than-air flight, which were telegraphed with fanfare across the US, was a state of existence that had seen little change since the Reconstruction after the Civil War. The U.S.'s history of treatment of its black citizens was at best stagnant and at worst horribly cruel. In fact, so successful was the Ku Klux Klan in terrorizing black voters that 85 years would pass between the elections of the first and second black senators. The Klan, which had disbanded in 1871, reformed in 1915 and spread a new wave of terror in the North, Midwest and South.

The government of white men often ignored or condoned acts of violence against Negroes. Many of the laws were designed to harass, segregate or make life more difficult for blacks. *Plessy v. Ferguson* (1896) condoned the euphemistic "separate but equal" racism that ruled blacks' lives until 1954 and beyond. Separate meant separate entrances (the back door), residences (the other side of the tracks), and bus seats (in the rear).

In spite of a history of suffering, the culture that slaves brought with them from Africa, mixed with the influence of European folk songs and forged into something all their own blossomed and grew. It was a rich mixture of pain and salvation, one that gave birth to Berry and continues with the Clash. Because of the Jim Crow (segregationist) laws, the gospel and blues songs remained underground in all-black clubs or church groups. A few of the venues, such as Harlem's Cotton Club, rivalled whites' best showcases for talent. But until radio came along, few whites were exposed to what was then called "race music."

Such was the state of the States when Charles Edward Anderson Berry was born in San Jose, California, in 1926. (Most biographers place the date at Jan. 15; Berry would say it was Oct. 26. It is only recently that he confirmed the year after claiming throughout his career that he was born in 1931.) His father, Henry, a carpenter, moved the family shortly afterwards to St Louis, Missouri, and later to Wentzville which became Chuck's life-long base.

Wentzville, a tiny town (about 3,000) with a large percentage of residents with German heritage, sits midway between St Louis and

Columbia, Mo., and Missouri is just about dead-center in the US. Even in St Louis, there was the separate, "colored" section of town called Elleardsville, where the Berrys lived. Their neighborhood, however, is most often described as middle-class, with trim lawns and neat houses. There Chuck would grow up with his two sisters and two brothers in a one-family house on Good Street.

Music was an important element in the Berry household. Both parents became active members of the nearby Antioch Baptist Church, where Henry sang bass and his wife, Martha, sang soprano. Of course they brought the children, and soon Chuck's sisters, Lucy Ann and Thelma, learned to sing and play piano. Chuck picked it up too, and made his debut in the church choir at the age of 6. Berry recalls, "The first music I can remember enjoying was way back in church. I was 4 years old and I was amazed by this particular song. It had this part that went . . . 'and we will WALK, WALK, WALK.' Each time they'd sing 'walk' the deacons would pat on the wooden floor. It jarred the whole church and got into me – that vibration from the floor."

In one BBC interview, Berry said his father's reading of rhymes to him was another early influence. And indeed, the only comment he's made since on the wonderfully image-laden lyrics of his songs was "I like to make 'em rhyme." Later Lucy Ann would become a leading contralto of a gospel group that toured the area. His brothers worked as contractors with their father.

St Louis, fifty miles away, a Southern city in spite of its Midwestern location, had already become a center for hybrid forms of music, by virtue of the turn of the century ragtime pianists, Tom Turpin and Scott Joplin. At the St Louis World's Fair, they led an incredible boom in syncopated dance rhythms. For many years, travelling black musicians had made it a regular stopover on their way up the Mississippi from New Orleans to Chicago, or on their way to California from the East Coast. These itinerant musicians, travelling in a Jim Crow car or beneath one, played the black night spots in town or went across the river to East St Louis, Illinois, a rough suburb. Like their blues songs, their lives were often made up of brushes with the law, ripoffs by managers, and the undercurrent of violence among themselves and as prey to the widespread sadism of racists.

There were, of course, blacks who prospered in spite of the times. Josephine Baker went from Harlem to become the rage of the Paris demi-monde. Louis Armstrong, the genius of New Orleans, kept an avid audience for over half a century. Some blues singers, like Roosevelt Sykes, led relatively uneventful lives. But all too often, with the life on the road came confrontations with The Man.

Texas blues guitarist Leadbelly escaped from one road gang and was later convicted of murder after he had spent many years travelling and playing with Blind Lemon Jefferson. Muddy Waters' guitarist, Pat Hare, Charley Jordan and Pine Top Smith also served time for homocide.

The blues musicians in and around St Louis at that time included William Bunch (a.k.a. Peetie Wheatstraw, the Devil's Son-In-Law and the High Sherrif of Hell), who sang and played both piano and guitar; his partner, Charley Jordan, Henry Spaulding and J.D. Short. In nearby Kansas City, the vastly influential Joe Turner kept the blues alive in local clubs and may have been heard on the Berrys' radio. Much of their blues was slow and lugubrious and their themes were women, money and liquor.

For many years, the Paramount and Okeh labels had put out the so-called "race" records which would become the base for rhythm & blues. Through the thirties and forties, black disc jockeys like Dogface, Lord Fauntleroy, Jet Pilot of Jive, Fatman Smith, Bonnie Prince Charlie Geter or Rockin' Lucky would build up their programs for the black audiences in urban surroundings. Also off the mainstream were the "hillbilly" records, a term coined by an Okeh executive.

It was during this period that the single most influential electric guitarist played. Charlie Christian, who performed and recorded with the Benny Goodman band for just two years (1939–41) before he died at the age of 22, accidentally stumbled on a new technology that influenced hundreds. Les Paul's purpose in attaching his pickup was to enable guitars to be heard over an orchestra, but he inadvertantly created a new sound by cutting off the high overtones that gave the acoustic its trademark. Christian, trying to recreate those tones, turned up the volume and bass on his Gibson amp. The amp responded by distorting with a dark, heavy, rough sound, and Christian put it to good use. Soon Chicago area musicians Muddy Waters and Hubert Simlin picked it up as well.

Berry's playing is remarkably similar to Christian's and he uses a Gibson as Christian did, though Chuck's ES–355 has a few extras: two humbucking pickups with separate pole pieces for each string, stereo wiring and a solid maple center running through a semi-hollow body.

Along with Charlie Christian came T–Bone Walker, whose nonchalant clowning while playing did nothing to hide his musical skill. Also by 1940, Louis Jordan, one of the few singers Berry has named as an influence, had formed his Tympany Five, and made smash hits of "Saturday Night Fish Fry," "Beware" and "Choo Choo Ch'Boogie." Jordan's approach was definitely light-hearted and fun; on the other hand, another Berry hero, the up and coming Nat King Cole, had a mellifluous, crooning style that Berry would forever envy. Berry later said, "If I had to choose an artist to listen to through eternity,

it would be Nat Cole. And if I had to work through eternity, it would be with Louis Jordan." Other artists Berry would name as influences are Les Paul, whose "How High the Moon" was a particular favourite, Christian Walker, Carl Hoagan and Glen Gray. He would describe his own singing as "Nat and (Billy) Eckstine with a little bit of Muddy." Surprisingly, though, he has said that he doesn't recognize his own style – just bits and riffs from all those who went before him.

Many of these singers Berry may have heard in his very early years at Simmons Grammar school, at home or at the homes of friends. In a *Rolling Stone* interview in which Berry fielded questions from a Berkeley student audience, he described his first experimentations with music, which began with the church choir: "The feeling to harmonize began to be a desire of mine; to get away from the normal melody and add my own melody and harmony was imperial, and I guess that grew into the appreciation for music."

At Sumner High School in the 40s, Chuck Berry met an age he loved so much he would never leave it. It was while he was in his teens that he bought a used Spanish 6–string guitar for $4.00. He also taught himself piano and sax and met the woman he would later say was his first, biggest influence – his music teacher at Sumner, Julia Davis, who had helped him learn guitar. And when he was a junior, he startled his All Men's Musical Review audience with a version of Joe Turner's "Confessin' the Blues". Amid the formal, upright songs that makes up the usual format for such an event, he must have impressed them enormously with those gut-bucket blues. Tom Stevens, an accompanying guitarist, also impressed Berry.

When he was 16, World War II broke out, and with it came a new sound and look. Big bands were bigger and wilder than ever, and bands like Spike Jones' brought an even higher degree of humor than had yet been heard. The attire for the most serious of draft-dodgers and ne'er-do-wells was the zoot suit.

When the war broke out, for teenagers still at home, it was a time of enormous activity directed towards a common goal, where a kid from Anytown, U.S.A., could come home a war hero, or, better yet, dance with Rita Hayworth at the Stage Door Canteen. Just as the remarkably silly movies of that time show, wartime for many of those high-schoolers could be . . . well, a lot of fun. And although Berry never entered the army, it was an experience he referred to time and again in songs and interviews, like so many other trappings of his high-school era.

In 1944, as the end of the war was in sight and the nation was preparing for the huge party when the boys came home, Berry was sent to reform school for an amateurish attempted robbery with two companions. He was 18 and would remain there for three years. Details about this event are sketchy at best, but it is more likely that Berry was temporarily broke or feeling stifled than

intending a career of crime.

When he was released, Berry found work on the factory line as an assembler at the General Motors Fisher Body plant, and began night school in what seems an almost schizophrenic negation of the life there – cosmetology at the Poro School of Beauty Culture. One can only imagine what it must have been like to spend days at a tough, macho auto body plant and nights styling hair. He may have followed his sisters there in the hope of meeting girls; at any rate, they all three got their licenses and became cosmeticians. Another early interest was photography.

Somewhere along this time he bought his first car, a '33 Ford, for $34, which took him three months to pay for. He also acquired a wife and two children, and by 1952, he sought to supplement his income from hairdressing by hiring out as a guitarist.

Berry had known pianist Johnny Johnson for about four months, so when Johnson asked him to replace a saxophone player in his Johnny Johnson Trio, he readily accepted. Johnson and Berry would form one of the great piano/guitar partnerships of pop music, and Johnson would prove nearly as influential in his own right as Berry. Chuck would later describe him as "born 30 years too late" and one of the all-time great boogie-woogie pianists. He would record with Berry throughout his career, and it is his inimitable, piano on "Maybellene" and most of the rest of Berry's hits that gave them much of their distinction.

For the next four years, they played as the Johnny Johnson Trio at house parties, church gatherings, and went onto play some of the East St Louis clubs like the Moonlight Bar, the Crank, and the Cosmopolitan Club, where they became something of a house band playing for about $14 a night. Within a year or two, they had become one of the most popular groups around with black audiences. The competition was tough–Little Milton, Albert King and Ike Turner were among those who regularly played in the area. Turner and Berry became hot rivals.

Bo Diddley, who was among the Chicago area musicians at about the same time, described those early gigs in liner notes from a recent compilation album: "Man, we played some smoky holes. Bars under the El station, in storefront clubs and it was hard, so hard you was looking for the worm to pull the *robin* into the ground, you dig?"

It wasn't until Berry took his songs to the Chess brothers in Chicago that his talent emerged as pre-eminent and the trio was renamed the Chuck Berry Combo, which began travelling around to push the records. "From then on, it was Chuck Berry all the way," said Johnson.

Probably the most influential events in Chuck Berry's life were those times when he climbed into his Ford and roared out of town with no particular place to go. With the exception of die-hard urbanites, almost any American over the age of 16 knows that his car is far more than a means of transportation. It's even more than the physical extension of his own body and personality. To a good number it was a home. They grew up in them as Dad wandered from town to town, transplanting them in one town and the next like so many potted geraniums. Many can recite the makes and models of the family's cars more easily than the various addresses they inhabited.

The 50s were the beginning of an era that is just now ending: cheap cars, cheap gas, and long, long, stretches of highway waiting for the test. Even now, after the advent of Gary Numan's alientated era of "Cars", kids still pile in and take the same soul—testing trek that lured Huck or even Chaucer's Canterbury pilgrims. Just for the sense of motion, the new faces, the new places.

There was plenty to tempt a young man from the 'burbs to all those places he'd read about in books, or even more important, heard over the radio. During these years before his success at Chess and after his release from reform school, Berry has said that he spent some time on the road "just hoboing ... San Francisco, New York, Chicago ... the coast-to-coast trip".

To a whole generation growing into their

cars, driving would become an occupation of sorts, with destinations even more vague than Berry's. Thousands of gallons of fossil fuel would be frittered away in the all-important teen hobby, "riding around". Cars were no longer the rich man's luxury – soon everyone could afford one of the huge half-ton Packards or Hudsons, whose somber black or dark green exteriors were turning the most astonishing shades of metalflake red.

Immortalized in *American Graffiti*, riding around had several purposes. Obviously, meeting the opposite sex was the underlying allure, but it was most important never to show that that was your exact purpose. You just happened to be driving around the pool for the 24th time that day, or you just had to have a cherry marshmallow vanilla ice with your pizza steak and the drive-in was the only place that had it. There you could relax as tunes blared over the speakers: the Drifters, the Coasters, Paul and Paula, Jerry Lee, Fats, Frankie Lymon and the Teenagers. When you got tired (or lucky) at the drive-in hamburger palace, you could cruise the main drag once more and go to the drive-in movies and, although he was married and had two daughters by the time he left the Poro School of Beauty Culture to become a cosmetician, Berry soaked in the importance of the phenomenon happening across the country and shared the same excitement of the times.

Today, we recognize the themes as American icons. Commercial as Coca-Cola, his songs are celebrations of the fast-food culture and conspicuous consumption that still comprise the US. Like Jack Kerouac and Allen Ginsberg, beat poets of the road, he was a documenter of sleaze. For the most part, he avoided political statements and simply recorded and celebrated adolescent American life. He explored every aspect of the car as symbol of sexual power, freedom and status. "No Money Down" ('56) is a gleeful catalogue of extras to order for a new Caddy (and, according to Wentzville residents, is an accurate description of the Cadillac in which he later swept through town).

The themes are a jumbled display of postcards from '55: sleek autos, young girls, jukeboxes, phones, roadmaps. And, especially since the rebirth of old-time rock & roll, the "girls and cars" songs remain the mainstay of pop.

But in those years up to '55, he continued to play with the Johnny Johnson trio in St Louis and the surrounding area. Ike Turner's presence had spurred more competition because he had a 16-piece band who could imitate almost any popular sound around. Suddenly instead of the usual pickup band's loose arrangements, there was a taste of the big time in St Louis' back yard. The climate, which was teeming with talent, prompted Berry to make another trip to Chicago to audition for Muddy Waters.

As with most of the events in Berry's life, there are conflicting versions of that famous trip. Maybe Berry's favorite is the one he told most often: after managing to get close enough

to Waters, Berry played some songs that impressed Waters enough for him to urge Berry to "go see Leonard" in Chicago. The very next day, he just happened to be walking in the neighborhood of the Chess offices (so says the back cover of *St Louis to Frisco*) and dropped in. There he was encouraged to come back with some of his own material. Struck with sudden inspiration, he rushed home to pen "Maybellene".

"It had never occurred to me to write my own songs," he told one interviewer.

The story is probably fairly close to what really happened, but other versions (which Berry also supplied) sound closer to the truth. It was his third such trip to Chicago, where he'd met Waters a year before. He took along Johnny Johnson, who testified that "Maybellene" and "Wee Wee Hours (chosen for their first single) were part of the band's reportoire long before the Chicago trip.

Reportedly the original name of "Maybellene" was "Ida Red" or "Ida Blue" and was a take-off of the up and coming rockabilly trend. The name "Maybellene" (to which it was changed at the suggestion of Leonard Chess) came, depending on what you read, from either a cow, a nursery rhyme or hair cream. (Johnson said it was the hair cream.)

Chess liked the four cuts Berry played for him: "Ida Red", "Wee Wee Hours", "Roll Over Beethoven" and "Too Much Monkey Business". Berry had recorded them with his band in his living room on a mono recorder. But Leonard suggested Berry give "Ida Red" a "bigger beat" and change the name. Chess then recorded the single with Johnson on piano, Leslie Dixon on bass, Jasper Thmas on drums and Bo Diddley's cohort Jerome Green on maracas on May 23, 1955.

Johnson was surprised that Chess chose to push "Maybellene" instead of the more bluesy "Wee Wee Hours".

"We thought 'Maybellene' was a joke y'know," he said in an interview with Bob Angell in *Music & Sound Output*. "People always liked it when we did it at the Cosmopolitan Club, but it was 'Wee Wee Hours' that we was proud of. That was *our* music."

A few weeks later, Chess took a demo of "Maybellene" to wildly popular DJ Alan Freed at radio station WINS in New York and told him to play it. Chess said in an interview with a *Ramparts* reporter: "The dub didn't have Chuck's name on it or nothing. By the time I got back to Chicago, Freed had called a dozen times saying it was his biggest record ever. History, the rest, y'know?"

Somewhere along the line, Freed managed to get a finger in the pie, along with DJ Russ Fratto–each accorded one-third of the royalties. It is possible that Freed heard a tape and made suggestions before a disk was pressed, but more likely Chess traded off the royalty for airplay. Recently Berry disclosed that although he'd managed to get the rights away from Fratto, Freed's estate still receives that one-third.

By July, the single was officially released and it streaked onto the charts. "Maybellene"

would go on to become the first-ever record to win *Billboard*'s Triple Crown, entering the pop, country and R & B charts.

It was quite an accomplishment for a song about hair cream written by a cosmetician.

"A Cadillac rollin' on the open road
Nothin' outruns my V–8 Ford..."

The song caught all the speed and excitement of a local drag race with the added allure of the woman who done him wrong. "Motorvating" is probably the best way of describing the searing urgency of Berry on guitar and Johnson on piano.

"Wee Wee Hours", on the flip side of the release was a good tune too, but the kids wanted the big beat, cars and young love. "It was a trend and we jumped on it," said Leonard Chess.

Everyone else jumped on it too. The first indication Berry had was the next week, on August 1, when a Jack Cook from the Gale Agency presented Berry with a contract. " 'You got a hit, sign here,' " Berry said Gale told him. Gale was Berry's first and only manager, and he didn't last long. For the rest of his career, Berry would manage himself.

Berry kept his cosmetician's booth until, he said, he "got a contract for $400." "Maybellene" broke after he'd been a hairstylist for about six months.

The following year after "Maybellene" was a gruelling one, with Berry and his band accepting a contract tour that circled them from New York to Florida and back again. On August 9, Berry played what he called his "first professional gig" at Gleason's in Chicago and went from there to Youngstown, Ohio. The tour would be an astounding 101 dates in 101 days.

"Whew, the feeling it was to go from nothing to top bill in a few weeks, I could never explain," said Johnson.

From that time on, Berry would make sure he would never have to go back to a life from payday to payday again. He took full advantage of the head start "Maybellene" gave him and in the following year would release a string of hits whose influence reverberates still. Johnson and the rest of his band didn't see much of Berry in those days, he said, because Chuck spent so much time in his room, up until the bus left for a new gig, writing new songs.

The first release after "Maybellene" was "Thirty Days" backed by "Together." "Thirty Days" was a more traditional blues-inspired song, more like the material from the St Louis clubs. It created a bit of interest, but failed to show on the charts. But "Maybellene" started a routine for Berry that would go on for the next four years: "Write a song, tour with it, push it till you get a hit, write another, tour with it . . ."

In the meantime, the "real" world outside the endless circuit of clubs and halls Berry had begun to play was a sharp contrast to his own freewheeling life. The adults who survived the war to make up the clergy, business and government busied themselves with much

more important issues than rock & roll.

In March of 1950, Senator Joseph McCarthy had set the tone for the entire decade in a mere five and a half hour speech. The State Department, he claimed, was in truth a nest of some 81 (or 205 or 57; reports varied) Communists. So receptive was the American public to such an idea that he was stopped only after many careers were ruined and public figures humiliated at the hands of the House Un-American Activities Committee. It was then that Sen. Richard Nixon began to make a name for himself.

McCarthy did not, after all, have any proof, as he had repeatedly claimed. What he did have was uncanny political acumen. There was a large pool of paranoia out there, and he became famous putting it to ill use. On the exterior, the American public seemed stolid and no-nonsense: fashion of the day dictated shirts buttoned up to the adam's apple, skirts to the mid-calf, with layer upon layer of thick, drab cloth. Even the automobiles provided a heavy enough shield from the outside that they vaguely resembled A–bomb shelters.

Rigid uniformity was the rule, and when McCarthy came up with the handy catchphrase "Reds," suddenly the public had a term for anyone who differed and therefore threatened.

Rows of identical houses sprung up in ghastly suburban sprawls. Roles were neatly divided between male and female. Neighborhoods, churches, schools, and nightclubs were sharply divided between black and white. As if to avoid any confusion, rest rooms and drinking fountains bore signs reading "colored."

If he had come out in 1950, Chuck Berry and his comrades might have been burned as witches because the music of the era reflected the same suburban ideals: it was white, calming, upright, and did anything but rock the boat. In fact, up to the early 50s, the industry seemed to be trying to bring back the big band era without the jump: Percy Faith, David Rose, Henri Rene and others played lush varieties of Muzak. Guy Lombardo was a bit more daring – he played swing.

Up until the end of the war, the most powerful musical groups were the ASCAP (Association of Songwriters, Composers, Artists and Performers) which licensed songs for Broadway show tunes, and major labels' executives, of whom Mitch Miller was the figurehead. ASCAP and Miller considered R&B and country notoriously low-class and ignored the markets, leaving them to other, small companies. Here radio was to step in to form Broadcast Music Incorporated (BMI), which would handly licensing for those regional markets. Predictably, the men behind the ASCAP hated it, and their hatred grew in direct proportion to the number of records BMI artists sold.

The "other" record labels that had been left the slim pickings of the regional marketplace were in those days small companies, often family or individually owned. They operated in the midland cities of Chicago,

Nashville and Memphis, which were, not surprisingly, hotbeds of R&B.

Although it was in New York, the then-infant Atlantic label was typical of the independent record company that became a major force with the "race and hot jazz" catalog it created in the 50s. Ahmet and Nesuhi Ertegun, sons of a Turkish diplomat, remained in the USA to finish their education when their father returned home. Ahmet had taken to hanging around Washington's R&B clubs and knew many early blues artists from there. Hoping to earn a little side money while working on his Ph.D., he sold his extensive collection of jazz records to form Atlantic in 1947.

Soon, of course, the business became a full-time effort, but Atlantic's first hit, "Drinkin' Wine Spo-Dee-O-Dee" by Sticks McGhee in 1949, was only the first in a series that would prove the Erteguns' unerring sense of style. It also insured that Atlantic would stay afloat when big distributors were forced to take notice. (Distribution was a big problem for the independents, who often drove around selling 78s from the trunks of their cars.) The same year, Antoine "Fats" Domino released his first single, "The Fat Man" on another independent label, Imperial, drawing on his Dixieland-New Orleans background for the boogie-woogie piano style. The majors may have found the success of these "race" records a bit troubling, but they were easy enough to dismiss. On the horizon, however, DJ Alan Freed was stirring up a very large brouhaha.

Freed had begun as host of a classical program on WJW in Cleveland, Ohio, and he saw on a first-hand basis the wane of the majors' influence in the regional market. On a visit to a friend's records store, he was amazed by the numbers of white kids buying R&B records. He started buying them himself, and after about a week of listening and wondering, he returned and talked the station manager into allowing him to DJ a rhythm and blues show. The manager agreed, but to avoid any stigma, Freed named the show "Moondog's Rock & Roll Party." It was the first time the term had described a kind of music, although "rocking" had variously described a kind of hand action on boogie piano, having a real good time, and screwing.

In 1951, Sam Phillips had not yet formed his own company, but was working at the Memphis Recording Studio as an engineer. He was also working as a talent scout for Chicago-based Chess records, and contributed to the recording of Jackie Brenston's "Rocket 88" on that label. Many rock historians point to "Rocket" as the first rock & roll record; some others (such as Greil Marcus in *Mystery Train*) to Phillips' work with Harmonica Frank.

Phil and Leonard Chess, two Polish immigrants, formed their label, then called Aristocrat, in 1947. By 1949, when they changed the name to Chess, they had already become specialists in race records. They had begun in the business as managers of some blues clubs, like their Macamba Lounge, where a singer named Andrew Tibbs was gigging when a Hollywood agent came in. Tibbs had attracted good word of mouth, so the agent dropped in. Leonard Chess, the more active of

the two brothers, decided then and there to act. Tibbs was the first to record on Aristocrat. (According to some sources, southern distributors reacted so negatively to the association of blacks and aristocrats that Leonard chose the family name to avoid conflict.)

In the next few years, the Chess brothers made good use of their base and signed much local talent. Among them were Muddy Waters, Howlin' Wolf, Little Walter, Sonny Boy Williamson, the Flamingoes and the Moonglows. Ike Turner, Berry's rival in St Louis, who had played guitar on "Rocket 88", was responsible, as talent scout, for finding many of those singers. The Chess label was a stronghold of R&B, and so influential that the Rolling Stones later cut a single as a tribute to the firm, "2120 S. Michigan Ave.," their address. Chess' second release and their first hit was Muddy Waters' "Rollin' Stone", which spawned the name of that group, Bob Dylan's "Just Like a Rollin' Stone" and *Rolling Stone* magazine.

By the time Berry travelled to Chicago to find the Chesses, there was already a well-beaten path. Great pianists like Otis Spann, Henry Gray and Lafayette Leake were Chess stalwarts, as well as bass player Willie Dixon, all of whom later played on Berry records.

In the same year that Berry took his demos to Chess, Bo Diddley took his demo versions of "I'm a Man/Bo Diddley" there, and Chess released his first single a few months later. Mississippi-born Diddley (a.k.a. Ellas McDaniel) spent much of the early 50s in Chicago clubs and undoubtedly met Berry then. Berry's "No Money Down" owes much to "I'm a Man."

Some of the singers Leonard Chess signed were quite open in their opinion that the man had little or no taste in music. Singer Etta James (signed in 1960) described in an Oct. 11, 1973 *Rolling Stone* interview recording sessions in which Leonard would accompany James to the recording booth and pinch or punch her ("I mean literally *punch* me") to coax what he thought would be appropriate screams or yowls from her. "Whatever tune had the most 'ooch' or 'eech' or whatever, that's the one he thought was going to be a hit," she said. James also said Leonard "didn't know A from Z in a beat" and would carefully watch for James' foot to begin to tap while listening to takes. Then he would begin tapping himself and proclaim, "That's it! That's going to be a hit record! Believe what Leonard tell you!"

Marshall Chess, Leonard's son who took over the business after his father died and later went on to form Rolling Stones Records, said his father had no pretensions about having great taste, or even as a great music lover. He told Peter Guralnick in *Feel Like Going Home*: "My father was a music lover in a very strange way. People used to talk, they'd think he was some kind of freak because all he'd ever want to do was go to these little funky clubs that no white person would ever dream of going to, to hear new acts, to buy new talent. I don't think he ever thought of himself as a music lover. But he was in his own way."

Ahmet Ertegun of Atlantic said they developed some taste along the way. Whatever their talents, the Chess brothers contributed enormously to the development of rhythm & blues and rock & roll. Among their technical accomplishments were the first echo chamber (by hanging a mike in a bathroom for Junior Mance's "Foolish Heart"), and a sewer pipe hung from the ceiling created a tenth of a second delay. Other effects were completely accidental, or may have come from staff engineers like Willie Dixon, Phil Chess admitted later.

Perhaps the most momentous occasion of 1951 was a record that failed to show on the charts. Bill Haley, who had released a number of traditional country & western tunes with his Saddlemen, changed the backup group's name to the Comets and covered "Rocket 88" on Essex. In spite of the record's poor showing, the experience so intrigued him that he decided to try it again.

Decca later bought Haley's contract, probably more for his country & western sound than any taste for rockabilly. As quoted in Charlie Gillet's *The Sound of the City*, Haley said, "The style we played in '47, '48, '49 was a combination of country and western, Dixieland, and old style rhythm and blues. I felt that if I could take a Dixieland tune and drop the first and third beats and accentuate the second and fourth, and add a beat the listeners could clap to as well as dance, this would be what we were after.

All the basic ingredients were there to inject life into the airwaves, but it would take a few years for the big band syndrome to burn itself out. Audiences were still timorous. However, Haley's "Rocket 88" was the first sign of the convergence of the two regional markets that would give rock its real boost, and the men who would catapault it – Freed, Phillips and the rest – were already set.

The other half of the ignored marketplace, country & western, had also done well enough without the majors. Stars like Patsy Cline, Kitty Wells, the young Loretta Lynn and Hank Williams were making names for themselves, many on indie labels. In Lynn's case, she and her husband did the selling-from-the-trunk-of-the-car themselves, driving from one radio station to another to promote her first single. Undoubtedly, though, the most influential was Hank Williams, whose yodelly "You Cheatin' Heart," "I'm So Lonesome I Could Die," and "Why Don't You Love Me Like You Used to Do" were nothing if not white men's blues.

The center for those performers was Nashville, Tennessee, where the Grand Ole Opry and its live radio broadcasts had entertained country fans for nearly two decades. But by the mid-50s, the businessmen there were believing their own PR. It was Music City, USA, but if a musician's songs failed to come under a recognizable Nashville category, they would most likely be ignored. So many were turned away that an entirely new base for music was formed in the same state, in Memphis.

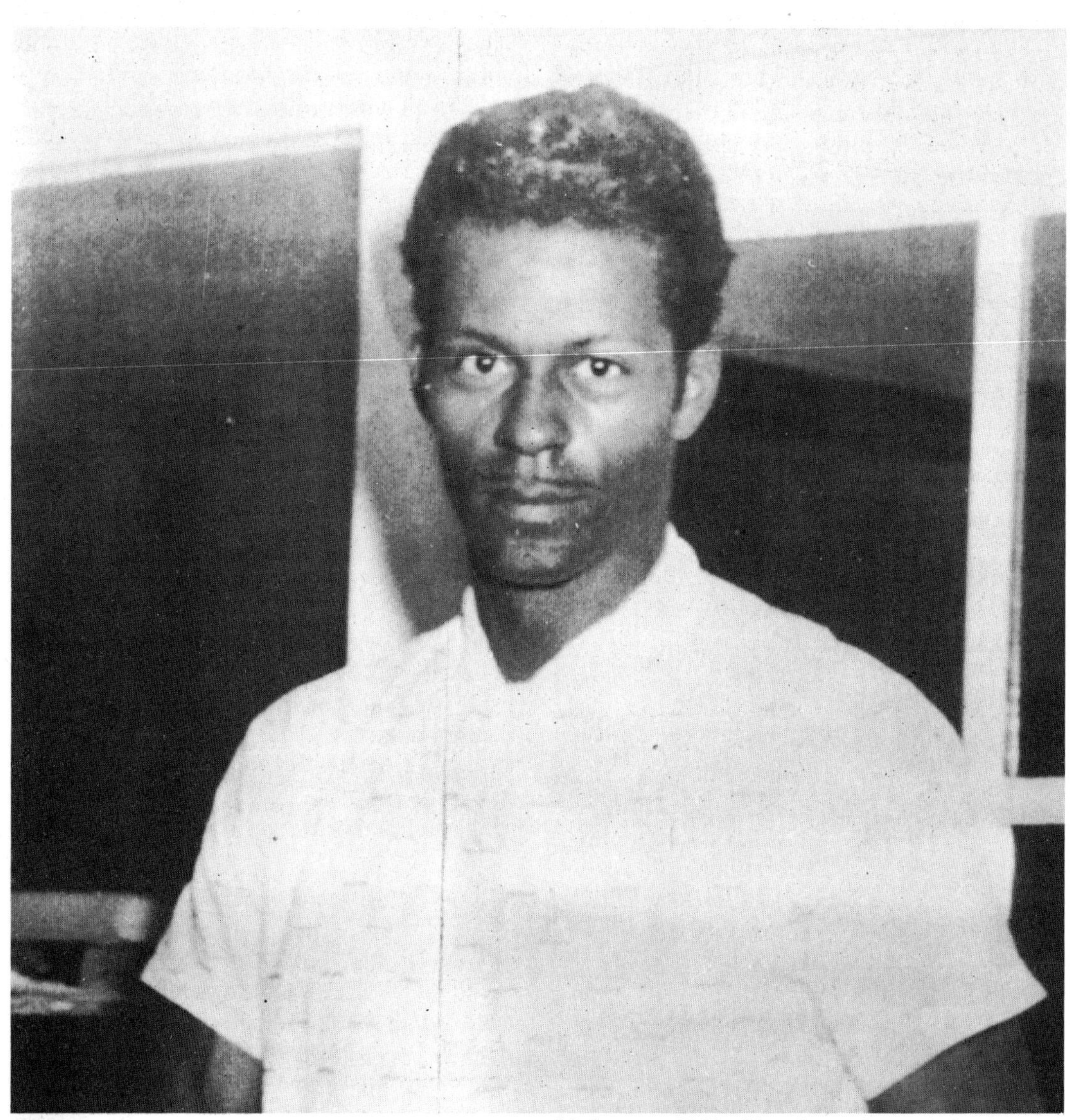

28 August 1959. Chuck awaits questioning on charges that he tried to date a Mississipi white girl.

Long before, Memphis' Beale Street had become a sort of nationwide main street for itinerant blues musicians, a notorious site of violence and tatty liquor stores, as well as a red-light district that featured some of the best piano playing around. Memphis, like St Louis and Chicago, had been an R&B center for years and Sam Phillips' location there dictated what he was to record. Close to Nashville and in the center of a blues home base, he heard the two types of music from the time he was very young. So, too, did Elvis Presley, who had moved with his family from Tupelo, Mississippi. First moved by the blues when he heard them in Tupelo as a child, Presley was anxious to become a singer and very willingly submitted to Phillips' tutelage.

What motivated Phillips to take this boy under his wing, was, of course, his famous search for the white man who could sing like a black. Phillips thought Presley had potential, so he groomed him for several months with hillbilly bandleader Scotty Moore. Moore was a part of the house band that Phillips kept on hand to back the singers he brought in, and they worked well in both blues and country. Elvis' voice may have been rooted in Tupelo blues, but his hair was the slicked-back mane of a red-neck truck driver.

Later, Robert Palmer quoted Phillips in *Jerry Lee Lewis Rocks*!: "At that time, you know, the three categories of music – pop, country music, rhythm & blues – were just miles apart, and yet, if you took a Southern country person and a Southern black, they were so damn close together. Still, that line came right down." Sometimes the line was more than just an idea. Chess A & R man Ralph Bass described the happenings at Haney's Big House to Michael Lydon in *Rock Folks*. Haney's was a black club which at first allowed no whites, then instituted a practice of selling "white spectator tickets" which were more expensive and usually in a far-off corner with no chairs or room for dancing. In the early 50s, they started having "white nights" or would stretch a rope across the dance floor. "The blacks on one side, whites on the other digging how the blacks were dancing and copying them. Then, hell, the rope would come down and they'd all be dancing together."

Phillips sold Presley's contract to RCA Victor for an estimated $35,000 in 1956. (A few years earlier, he had tried to sell his entire roster of artists, including Elvis, to Chess. Phil Chess said they refused because "we didn't consider ourselves a hillbilly label".) But Phillips' Million Dollar Quartet of Elvis, Jerry Lee, Carl Perkins and Johnny Cash would make a lasting impression on the music of the coming decades.

It's been noted often that Berry was somehow the converse of Elvis. Presley was the country kid singing the blues; Berry was the black singing country. A few years later, Berry would write a lightly sad "Memphis, Tennessee" that encapulates the bluesy-rockabilly style that makes the city.

Meanwhile, Bill Haley was still experi-

menting, and came up with a hit when he penned "Crazy Man Crazy" in 1953, which showed on the Hot 100 chart. "Shake, Rattle and Roll", a cleaned-up version of a Joe Turner song (Haley had deleted the reference to bed from the original) followed in '54. In 1955, his "Dim Dim the Lights" became the first rock & roll record by a white to show up on the black R&B charts.

Another Haley song of that same year, "Rock Around the Clock," was released without much success. Written by 63-year-old ASCAP member Max Freedman expressly to crack the youth market, the song languished until an event of the following year, the release of *Blackboard Jungle*, a movie about the decadence and danger at an urban high school starring Glen Ford, Sidney Poitier and Marilyn Monroe. (Miss Monroe barely escaped ravishment.) In the movie, the teacher (Ford) brings in a collection of his jazz records to show his empathy and they laugh him out of school. *Bill Haley* was *it*, man, the *end*, you twerp! (In the novel on which the movie was based, the kids threw out his jazz records and went back to what was *really* hip – Vaughn Monroe.) Once the movie was released, rural and suburban kids saw what urban kids were up to and that they weren't far apart.

What followed was sudden and absolute monarchy for Haley. It was a short reign before the more physically appealing Elvis took over, but with the release of *Blackboard Jungle* came riots (so they were described – they consisted mostly of excitable suburbanites dying for a look at their idol) in New Jersey. The flash of recognition was instant in London as well, and soon there were furrowed brows of concerned parents on the other side of the ocean as well. Haley was received in even more incredible throngs there, where he remains an idol, much more so than in the US.

Unlike the US, the UK had just one radio station – the BBC – that was definitely *not* top-40 oriented. The only radio station Londoners could hear that played rock & roll in the 50s was Radio Luxembourg, which was woefully crackly and indistinct. Later, Radio Caroline, a pirate station whose source was a ship, provided some alternative before it was raided and closed down. But besides the very few import records and the slight exposure from Radio Luxembourg, there was one other alternative. Author Hugo Williams, whose book *No Particular Place to Go* describes his travels in the US, said that one other way to hear the records was to go to the old-style record shops, which always included "listening booths" for its customers. "Of course, you never had any money to actually buy the records," said Williams, "so you'd be endlessly wheedling some poor clerk to play them for you. He'd put it on, and you'd dance in the booth, and then you'd have to come out and pretend you didn't like it."

Despite the fact that it was an underground movement for over eight years, rock & roll took root in the UK and produced fanatics that rivalled (and eventually outdid)

those in the US.

In 1957, when there were still passenger lines from the US, people like John Lennon and Paul McCartney heard Berry via the so-called "Cunard Yanks", sailors on passenger ships who were known for their flashy New York clothes. Along with the tassled, hand-painted pillows and ashtrays, they brought records by the then-unknowns Presley, Little Richard and Chuck Berry. Port cities like Liverpool were very receptive – the working class was much the same in both countries.

The generation who had suffered through World War II now had to endure this. It was almost too much. But once wartime pressures were off, kids were free to do pretty much as they pleased as long as they kept clean, did their homework and stayed away from Negroes. Prosperity had given kids money (the better to buy records with), technology gave them sleek cars, free enterprise had given them the drive-in, food additives and puberty had given them acne – there was much to bind the average teens to one another.

Paranoia was still obviously a guiding factor in the 50s. McCarthy was condemned by the senate in late '54, but the forces that brought him to power still existed. If the backlash that occurred after the initial mandate to integrate the schools was loud, messy and violent, it would calm down only to reincarnate in a more low-key, insidious forms of authority.

Among the songs that were released in 56: "Roll Over Beethoven," an unabashed rallying cry to the burgeoning sounds of rock & roll. "Go ahead, turn in your graves," Berry seemed to be saying, not to the literal dead, but to the zombies who walked and warned of the dangers of rock music. The B side is "Too Much Monkey Business," a perfect capsulization of the distracted state of adolescence. "Go to work, go to school . . . "Berry's chant would give rise to others, like Bob Dylan's "Get sick, get well, hang around the ink well . . ."

"No Money Down" and "Brown-Eyed Handsome Man" were others released that year, and the latter, like Berry's "Promised Land," was one of his few songs about being black in the US. "Havana Moon," which followed, was one of the first calypso songs, predating even Harry Belafonte.

On the music industry front, rock & roll was increasingly hard for the majors to ignore. They found a suitable substitute for ignoring the music by having some of their "house" singers cover the up-and-coming R&B hits. Dot became particularly notorious for this practice, which usually ended up robbing the original black artist of a hit. Squeaky clean, white-buck clad Pat Boone scored in the early years with a Chess number, the Flamingoes' "I'll Be Home" and later took Little Richard's "Tutti Frutti" and "Long Tall Sally" as well as Fats Domino's "Ain't That a Shame" high into the charts. The McGuire Sisters covered the Moonglows' "Sincerely" on Decca, the Crew Cuts made a huge hit from the Chords' groundbreaking "Sh-Boom." Georgia Gibbs would

Overleaf: A scene from *Rock, Rock, Rock*

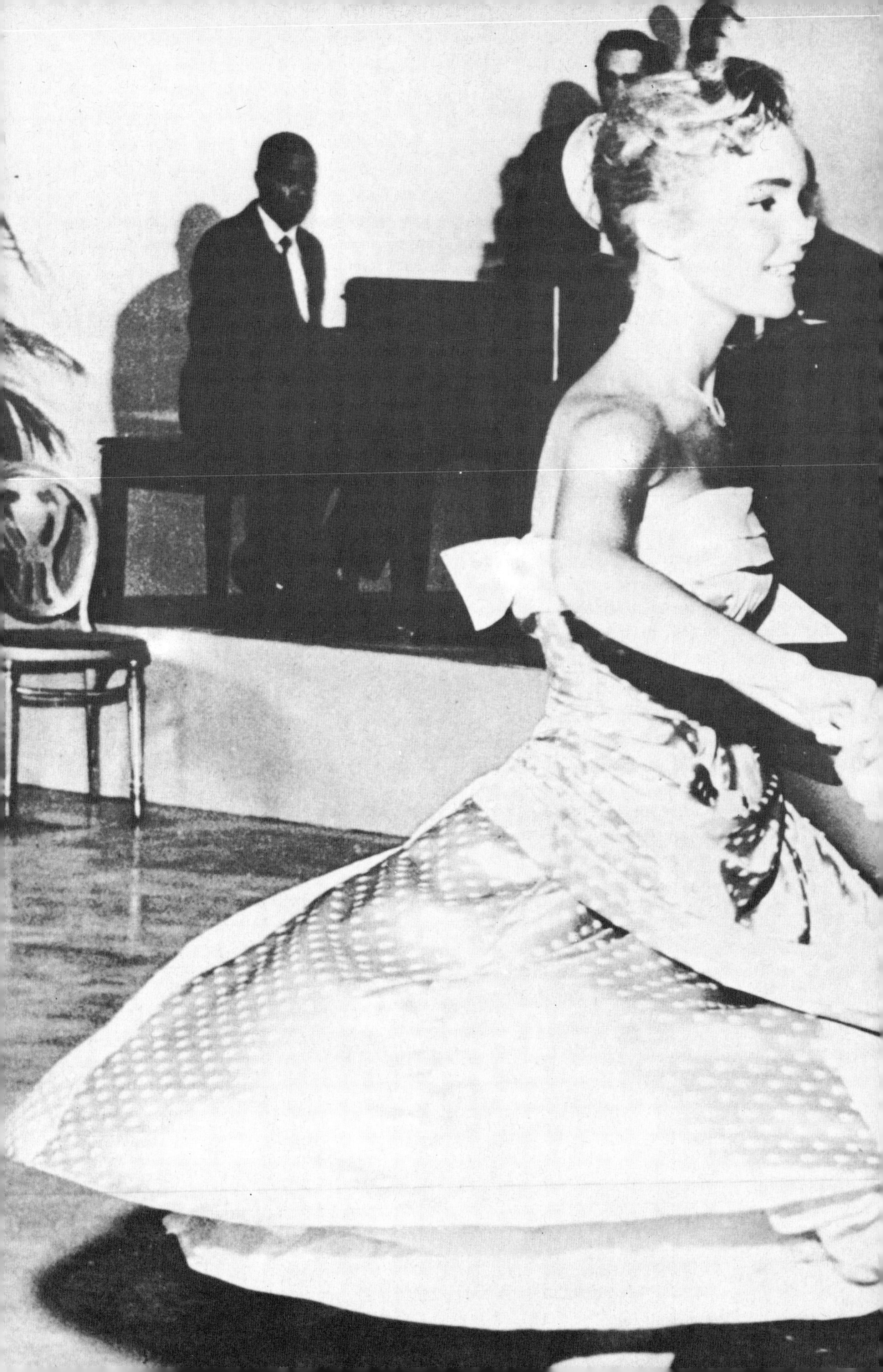

cover LaVern Baker tunes. Sometimes the artist would change the lyrics, as Haley had done with "Shake, Rattle and Roll". Boone changed "Long Tall Sally" slightly so that it wouldn't seem he was actually interested in more than one girl at the same time.

On the other hand, Alan Freed, as an easily identifiable leader of rock & roll, was coming under fire both for mixing the races at his live shows and the lewdness of the songs he played. It may have started with "Laundromat Blues" by the Five Royals ("Her machine is full of suds... it will cost you thirty cents a pound ..."), followed by even more blatant "It Ain't the Meat It's the Motion" (the Swallows); of course *everyone* knew what "Work with Me, Annie" really meant, especially when it was followed by "Annie Had a Baby" (Five Royals). Bullmoose Jackson had a song that began "She just loves my big ten-inch... record of her favourite blues". Others were "Bip Bam (Thank You Ma'am)" by the Drifters, "Ride Helen Ride" by the Hollywood Flames, and "Let Me Bang Your Box" by the Toppers. "People were so innocent then. They played 'Let Me Bang Your Box' for *weeks* before people caught on and took it off," said one Freed fan. "But of course they really knew."

Even Bo Diddley's "I'm a Man" and Chuck's "Reelin' and Rockin" pale in comparison to the audacity of those early pioneers. Luckily most parents couldn't understand the words. But Berry was more daring than most, and he represented a threat.

Already the KKK were busy behind the scenes with flyers and pamphlets warning parents not to let their children buy "nigger records". There was a motion on the floor of the Congress to determine if rock & roll might be a Communist plot. Economist Vance Packard would later testify that it was.

The worst fears of Middle America were fuelled by an event that newspapers labelled a "riot". Allan Freed decided to hold Moondog's Coronation Ball, his first live show, in Cleveland in 1952 featuring a full bill of R&B performers at the city's 10,000-seat arena. Reports vary on exactly how many turned up, but most likely it was 18,000. (Charlie Gillet gives 30,000; another states that 80,000 showed up.) Many whites showed along with the mostly black crowd, and the event was cancelled.

Once in New York, Freed, undaunted, started working as a promoter again and put on a series of shows at the Paramount theaters in Brooklyn and Times Square, regularly featuring Chuck, Fats Domino, Jerry Lee Lewis, Frankie Lymon and the Teenagers and the Coasters. The kids who saw them still remember.

"It was something you had to lie to your parents about," said Suzanne Feltzen, who did just that when she was about 16 years old. "They thought those shows were really bad. And they were! People would go crazy! They used to unscrew the lightbulbs from the fixtures and smash them... And of course, there were black kids there, and that was no good."

"Yeah, they were really wild," agreed

Tad Richards, who had travelled from Woodstock, New York, to attend the Times Square shows. "The first time I ever saw a guy put his hand down a girl's pants was at the Paramount."

By 1958 the series of shows had become a cause for concern that merited an article in the Sunday magazine section of the New York Times titled "Why They Rock 'n' Roll – And Should They?" Writer Gertrude Samuels described the big beat as a "tense, monotonous beat that often gives rock 'n' roll music a jungle-like persistence". The article also posed the question: "Is this generation of teenagers going to hell?" One sociologist concluded that the hysteria at the Paramount shows was "our fault. We haven't stirred the children with something to live by, to worship, to put their hopes in . . . Perhaps we have taken the glamour out of the good life . . ."

The Labor Day show at Brooklyn's Paramount in 1956 for some 6,000 would be a landmark of rock & roll because it was the first time Berry performed his famous duck walk. The move has become a standard Berry feature, his trademark in a way, and he claimed that it all happened by accident.

He'd always had the band looking sharp – it was something St Louis area musician Gabriel Hearns remembered about him. "His music had a zing to it nobody else had. And professional – he made his guys wear uniforms and be real neat. Chuck was always a perfectionist . . ." And when he told a Berkeley audience about the Paramount performance, the uniforms were of tantamount importance.

"I had to outfit my trio, the three of us, and I always remember the suits cost me $66, $22 apiece. We had to buy shoes and everything . . . anyway, when we got to New York, the suits, they were rayon but looked like seersucker by the time we got there . . . so we had one suit, we didn't know we were supposed to *change.* So we wanted to do something different, so I actually did that duck walk to hide the wrinkles in the suit – I got an ovation, so I did it again, and again, and I'll probably do it again tonight."

The move knocked 'em out, all right, and it still does. Berry displayed a natural grace and agility that made the average kid then green with envy, and at 56, his moves still seem effortless. They are the kinds of moves typical of youth's seeming ability to defy gravity – they represent somehow that unconscious but utterly confident assurance that one can do anything. They were like Elvis' gyrations – if you could dance, it would be like Elvis. If you could play guitar, it would be like Chuck, making it talk better than you could ever speak, but not limiting the interpretation to your fingertips, letting it take over your whole body instead.

The event closing this era was the first of a series of appearances Berry would make on Dick Clark's *American Bandstand,* which was based in Philadelphia. The two got in a terrific argument because Clark made everyone lip-synch their latest record rather than actually sing it live. Chuck told him "Chuck Berry is

not gonna open his mouth and have nothing come out." But in the end Leonard talked him out of his anger and Berry did lip-synch like the rest of them.

It was still the very early days of rock, but the deterioration had already begun. Elvis Presley was breaking the charts wide open with three of his songs, leading off with "Love Me Tender" as number one. The RCA Victor versions showed a huge difference from the Sun recordings. Presley was going for a wider audience with this smooth pop sound and he was getting it. Hero worship knew no bounds; girls fainted and were carried out of concerts in hysterics.

It was, of course, slightly different for Berry: as loose as the kids were getting, the girls knew enough to refrain from throwing themselves at a black man. And, with the exception of, perhaps, Michael Jackson, it's hard to think of a black singer who has ventured any closer to the teen idol with universal appeal than Berry did in the 50s. But in turn, his popularity paved the way for many others, convincing record executives that whites would buy black records.

It is impossible to say when Berry first began his stringent business policies, but promoter Richard Nader said Berry once told him a story to explain why he took only cash. A woman in Fayetteville, North Carolina called, asking him to come out for a fee of some $750. Berry drove in from St Louis in a rain that lasted all night. He finally arrived, to find a run-down ice cream shop behind the woman's house and a crowd of about 20 kids. But he went ahead and played the gig. Afterwards, he asked the woman for the money he'd been promised. She handed him a list on which she had recorded all her "expenses". "She had everything down there, down to the light bulbs," Nader says Berry told him. She claimed them as deductions from her profit, and after she'd finished her calculations, she offered Berry $1.75.

He told her to keep the money. All the way home in the rain to St Louis, Nader said, Berry told himself, "Never again." From then on, it would always be cash and always up front.

Nineteen fifty-seven has been singled out by many as a halcyon year for Chuck Berry, and his amazing success carried over into '58 and '59. He was a very busy man. His first movie effort, *Rock Rock Rock*, was released. It was one of a series of blockbusters based loosely on the format of Alan Freed's Paramount shows. *Rock Rock Rock*, was buttressed by the formidable powers of the Moonglows, the Flamingoes, a rare bit of footage of the Johnny Burnette Trio, LaVerne Baker, and Frankie Lymon and his Teenagers. Tuesday Weld made her debut in the picture, with Connie Francis supplying her vocals. Another Freed release of the same year featuring Freed as *Mr Rock & Roll* listed Berry in the credits, but he was cut from most copies.

Go Johnny Go, the title taken from the chorus of Berry's song, was his last release of the 50s, and, like *Don't Knock the Rock* and *Mr. Rock & Roll*, it centered on the story of a DJ, some white kids, and some "new talent" that was sure to stand the town on its ear. The crowd in that picture included Freed, Eddie Cochran, Jimmy Clanton, Ritchie Valens (in his only movie appearance), Harvey of the Moonglows, Jo-Ann Campbell, The Flamingoes, the Cadillacs, and Jackie Wilson.

Going to Hollywood to be in the movies was something Berry definitely counted as a major event in his career if one interprets songs like "Johnny B. Goode" autobiographically. "Bye Bye Johnny," "B. Goode"'s sequel, is all about Goode's mom sending him off to

Alan Freed in a scene from *Rock, Rock, Rock*

tinseltown. "Bio" refers to the movies, too.

Once he got out there, though, the actual movie-making process puzzled him. In one interview he described a scene in which the camera loomed within inches of his face and how boring he thought repeating the script was once he'd already read it. But the idea of being in the movies obviously appealed to Berry, and in his songs they are regarded with the same awe a teenager holds for the idol-makers.

The rock movies gave a further push to the movement, and for an artist like Berry, they were particularly important. For the first time, the kids could actually *see* their heroes, and since Berry's moves are such a vital part of his act, he would become a popular choice for movie-makers throughout his career.

By mid-1957, there were fully 25 major motion pictures devoted to rock & roll, and besides the easily apparent visual and cultural contribution they made, writers Phillip Jenkinson and Alan Warner note in *Celluloid Rock* that there were other, technical advances. They directly link the fine aural quality on *Rock Around the Clock* and other early films, a sound distinctly different from vinyl recordings, with the "wall of sound" techniques that would bring the Ronettes to fame in the 60s. Men like Phil Spector "produced their records like sound men rig a film studio for a production number . . . Some of the most exciting albums of the fifties and sixties were produced by men who thought in terms of time and space; a visual filmic experience transferred to a monaural slab of wax." The writers attribute such production techniques as dubbing, overlaying, treble and quadruple tracking, re-recording and re-mastering to the lessons record producers learned from these movies.

The next two years produced the body of Berry's most lasting songs. His singular most popular tune of that era, "School Days," was an anthem that still stands on sturdy legs today. It spoke immediately to the kids and their everyday, all-consuming concern, school, down to the last detail of the "guy behind you won't leave you alone". The song is a catalog of the waiting everyone went through, up to lunch and the crowded cafeteria until you're "out of the school and into the street," marked by the jubilant cries issued from the juke joint down the block: "Hail, hail, rock & roll . . ." to the youth of today's *real* concerns: Let's dance and make romance. Like "Maybellene," it was delivered in the same crisp diction and the wealth of detail was more than convincing. Berry wrote it at the age of 30, in the Street Hotel, a black hotel in downtown St Louis.

Another release of that year, "Oh Baby Doll," also became a favorite for ardent fans, along with "La Juanda", a further exploration of Latino rhythms, but failed to show on the charts. His third release of 1957, however, "Rock & Roll Music," would be an often-covered rave-up, laying the tracks for a genre of songs with rock music as its subject.

The following year was just as productive in terms of releases, among them a whole

array of hits. The first single was the seminal "Sweet Little 16," which may be the first acknowledgement of groupies, or simply the "weekend warrior" existence many kids led, with a wild life that turns dull once school is back in session. "They'll be rockin' on Bandstand, Philadelphia, Pa.," – once again Berry's ear was tuned to what was happening with Dick Clark's then-locally syndicated *American Bandstand*. The B side was a decidedly staid version of "Reelin' and Rockin", although he was known to treat audiences to the bawdy version even in these early days.

Next came the theme song most associated with Berry's life – "Johnny B. Goode", which was backed with "Around and Around". The parallels between Goode and Berry are too obvious to ignore, and Berry has said in an interview with Patrick Salvo that the original version of "the little country boy" had been the "little colored boy". "Goode" probably comes from the St Louis street where Berry grew up.

There followed another four singles in '58, starting with "Beautiful Delilah," the classic "Carol," "Sweet Little Rock & Roller," "Jo Jo Gunne," and his least commercially successful single, "Merry Christmas Baby" b/w "Run Rudolph Run". But a *Billboard* reviewer made no bones about his love for Berry's Christmas disc. "It's no secret at all that the Berry record fractured the *Billboard* review panel and had them stomping around the record room like few records have done."

It wasn't until this year that Chess released his first album, *After School Session*, followed by *One Dozen Berry's* in the same year. (The name, unfortunately, was a sign of things to come – several album titles would be plays on the name Berry.)

For the next three years, Berry was the only star to perform in all three of the "Biggest Show of Stars" series. The first, "The Stars of '56," headlined by Fats Domino, consisted of one hundred and one one-nighters, straight. Pianist Johnny Johnson said that more often, the routine was more like four days of travel and three in a hotel. In the following year, Berry and his group were signed for "The Biggest Show of Stars for '57" by Irwin Field. This was an 80–day cross country tour with Fats Domino, Bill Haley, Frankie Lymon and his Teenagers, the Drifters, the Everley Brothers (who would soon become Berry favorites), Paul Anka, LaVerne Baker, Clyde McPhatter, Jimmie Bowen, and the new group Buddy Holly and the Crickets. They travelled together for two and a half months, opening in Pittsburgh on Sept. 6 and playing anywhere they could. Average ticket prices for this outstanding group was $2–3. Buddy Holly's biographer, John Goldrosen, described a scene in the back of the tour bus showing Berry and Holly shooting craps with their night's earnings. They would play over 100 dates together, according to Berry. Holly recorded "Brown-Eyed Handsome Man" and "That's My Desire," one indication of his respect for Berry's songwriting prowess.

On another of these tours, Carl Perkins,

who'd set down the words to "Blue Suede Shoes" on a potato sack in his kitchen one early morning, was part of the talent lineup. He chose to follow the tour bus in his cadillac, and described how much Berry liked to get off the bus and ride in his Caddy. Perkins described with pride how Berry had set down the words to "Brown-Eyed Handsome Man" in the back seat, the words flowing out with no apparent difficulty. Another tour promoted by Freed would take the Crickets, Berry, Jerry Lee Lewis, and Frankie Lymon on a six-week jaunt through the countryside.

Life on a tour bus has been romanticized by the cinema, but the everyday routine of it must have been gruelling, to say the least. Anyone who has taken such a trip by bus knows how quickly the debris accumulates to ankle-depth, with bottles rolling from side to side as the bus takes a turn. Then there is the never-ending diet of junk food, the tempers growing shorter as the tour grows longer, the lack of sleep brought on by constant travel. Berry made up for the deficiencies as soon as he could by beginning a collection of Cadillacs that wowed the citizens of Wentzville whenever he tooled through, and later, getting a tour bus fitted with a custom interior which he called "Maybellene".

But of course there was to be more bad news for rock fans: Jerry Lee Lewis married his 13-year-old cousin, Myra, that same year. He encountered the wrath of the English on a

May tour there and was forced to return to the US after only two gigs, this in spite of his hit "Whole Lotta Shakin' Goin' On" which had flown to number one the year before. The Lewises were asked to leave their London hotel after Jerry Lee made the mistake of introducing Myra at a stage show.

Little Richard's exodus was even more bizarre and was the result of one or many harowing experiences, depending on whom you believe. One story has it that while he was sailing on Hunter River in Sydney, one of his band members taunted him, telling him to "prove his faith in God." In response, Little Richard tore several rings (valued at about $8,000) from his hand and threw the jewelry into the river, claiming he was through with the devil and would dedicate his life to God. According to Arnold Shaw's *The Rockin' 50s*, Little Richard enrolled in January 1958 at Oakwood College in Huntsville, Alabama, to begin his Seventh-Day Adventist indoctrination. He paid his four-year tuition in advance, and told a reporter, "If you want to live with the Lord, you can't rock & roll, too. God doesn't like it." He told another source he had a dream in which he "saw the world burning up and the sky melting with heat," and confessed that an experience in the Phillipines in which his plane temporarily caught on fire had been a spur; Specialty Records' Art Rupe was convinced there was another celestial signal involved: "He thought that the Sputnik was a sign from Heaven: that was it".

Then, too, was the tragic turn of events that took the lives of three of rock & roll's biggest talents in February 1959 when Ritchie Valens, the Big Bopper and Buddy Holly were killed in a plane crash just five miles from the runway. A year later, incessant travel again took its toll in a London taxi accident that claimed the life of Eddie Cochran and partially paralyzed Gene Vincent.

In August of '59, Berry had a scrape with the law that would prove to be an omen of things to come. The *New York Times* reported he'd been jailed in Meridian, Mississippi, for "trying to date a white girl". Berry said it was a misunderstanding stemming from a fan's boyfriend who got jealous when the girl approached Berry for an autograph. He was held without bail.

Still, Berry excaped major trouble through these years, despite a small complaint to the police from an Indian girl he'd taken under his wing that would take three years to drag through the courts before it was translated into yet another downfall – one tawdry enough to satisfy the ravings of an outraged public.

He remained amazingly prolific. He released four singles and two albums in 1959, including the hurdy-gurdy "Anthony Boy" (influenced by some Italian kids he'd met in Massachusetts). There followed "Almost Grown," which seems almost quintessentially 1959 with its chorus of doo-woppers in the background as Berry assumes the whiny voice of a teenager: "Don't bother us, leave us alone/Anyway, we almost grown". As a story of two teens who fall in love and marry, it's a prototype for "You Never Can Tell". After that came the classic "Memphis Tennessee" which Berry taped in his office with his secretary, Fran, on drums, and its B–side, "Back in the USA" with its unashamed patriotism. Berry wrote it after a visit to Australia that produced sharp pangs of homesickness once he found he couldn't order a hamburger or hot dog. "Broken Arrow/My Childhood Sweetheart" was the last release of '59.

The catastrophic events that had decimated the ranks of rock & roll were enough by themselves to provide a setback that would last until the rebirth with the Beatles and Rolling Stones several years later. Because the English had no equivalent of Alan Freed or Bob Horn or Dick Clark, there was very little backlash until the 60s and the "Would you let your daughter marry a Rolling Stone?" presented itself. There was perhaps an even more delicious aspect of the forbidden or underground because of the unavailability of many rock & roll disks.

It seemed that the same atmosphere here that had produced rock & roll to begin with – that old-time revivalism, coupled with shameless capitalism also produced a particularly insidious Calvinist streak that brought the brewing argument about tribal rhythms to the Congress of the US.

Up to the time of the Congressional investigations, what would become known as "payola" was not illegal. And it was obvious that some abuses occurred when certain labels' promo men met DJs. The promo men's job was to get their label's records on the air, and if the DJ seemed reluctant, the promo man's expense account might help alleviate any friction between them.

There were other elements involved in the investigation, which began in 1959 as a look into the charges against daytime television quiz shows. The corruption found there in the form of rigged contests and coached contestants was astounding. Then the investigation turned to radio. Said *Variety*: "ASCAP songsmiths ... take credit for switching the spotlight from TV quiz rigging to the disc jockey payola".

The ASCAP also had a strong ally in the form of adult public opinion. To many, rock & roll was an unsightly household mess that should be eradicated with industrial-strength authority, much as one put the living room in order with any number of the new labor-saving appliances. To them, it was the one intrusion in America (save those pesky Commies) that ruined a tidy, orderly world of Sunday church-going and unrelenting weekday avarice. The music was so far from their realm of understanding that when they wondered why their teenagers listened to the music, they began to suspect the source was the same that was bringing riots to their front door, the same source Mayor Daley would finger for the Chicago riots eight years later: Outside Agitators. (Probably Negro and certainly Communist.)

To many parents already teeming with self-righteousness, a mere phone call was enough. A single complaint from a parent could, in the early days, take a record off the air. Jerry Lee Lewis suffered most from this kind of treatment in the late 50s and early 60s.

Through '60 and '61, Berry continued releasing some great music although by then the Indian girl's complaint had blossomed into full-fledged court battles. "Too Pooped to Pop," an innocuous little ditty, was first, followed by "Bye Bye Johnny". Next came the instrumental "Mad Lad" and another car song, "Jaguar and Thunderbird". "Come On," probably the strongest release of those two years, features Martha Berry on vocals. (She also sang on "The Man and the Donkey" and "Trick or Treat".) "Come On" was his last release for two years.

Alan Freed was one of the first to suffer the effects of the payola investigations. Not only was he one of the most visible irritants in the eye of the public, but he had become one of the most highly paid DJs in the US. He earned $30,000 a year in regular salary, and totted up hefty profits in promotional gimmicks, royalties, and, of course, concert promotion, as well as record company payoffs. Just before the axe fell, Freed's Times Square Paramount Christmas show, a 12-day series, grossed over $300,000.

His first troubles came in the form of a run-in at a Jerry Lee Lewis concert in Boston when over-zealous police halted the show. Several people were badly injured before the

night was over, and Freed was charged with inciting to riot. When his station, WINS, refused to back him up on the charges (which were later dropped), Freed resigned and went to WABC. It was there he was presented with the standard form that was then being circulated stating he'd never taken payola. He refused to sign it, "on principle", and was fired. A few days later he was dropped from his rock & roll dance party on WNEW–TV. Freed then went to Los Angeles station KDAY, but trouble followed him there and in 1960 he was convicted of accepting $30,000 in payola. Two years later he was fined and given a suspended sentence; in 1964 he was charged with evasion of income tax. One year later, he was dead of complications brought on by alcoholism.

It was in this vindictive arena that Berry had to face trials in St Louis from '59 to '62. While touring in Mexico, he picked up a Spanish-speaking Apache girl and took her back to St Louis where he'd formed a nightclub. He gave her a job as a cigarette girl at the club, which was called Bandstand. After he fired her, the girl went to the police and told them her story. She was fourteen years old, and according to the police, Berry's actions constituted a violation of the Mann Act, sometimes called the "white slavery" law, meaning he had transported a minor across state lines for immoral purposes.

The first court date was ruled a mistrial after the judge's prejudices became apparent, referring to Berry as "this Negro". Berry pleaded innocent to the charges; his reason for bringing the girl to St Louis was to learn Spanish, he said – he was convinced that Spanish songs were the coming trend. She had told him she was 20.

In spite of the fact that it was revealed during the trial that the girl had been turning tricks at the hotel across the street from the club (which Berry didn't know), the second judge found him guilty and sentenced him to five years at the federal pen at Terre Haute, Ind. Although he would spend only two and a half years there, the kind of image it gave him was devastating. To be convicted of a sex crime in the fifties! One headline went "Rock & Roll Singer Lured Me to St Louis, Says 14–Year Old". Berry proved to be an easy mark for those looking for reasons to condemn rock & roll.

Amazingly enough, however, his conviction involving a 14-year-old girl wasn't as damaging as Jerry Lee Lewis' marriage to one. Lewis' career is only now recouping after that setback.

Berry may have actually been guilty, as the court decreed in 1960. But if it had been a white landowner in his place . . .

The two and a half years Berry spent behind bars in Terre Haute proved far more detrimental than Elvis' gig in the Army. When Berry was released in the fall of '63, the effects of his sentence were not at first clear. But it seemed he fell victim to delayed stress, according to those who'd known him both before and after the jail term. Carl Perkins noted the man who'd once seemed so friendly and easy-going was now terse and moody.

Nineteen-sixty three, the year Berry was released, was turbulent, but it would only be a sign of what was to come for the rest of the decade. In June, the Supreme Court decided that rules requiring the recitation of the Lord's Prayer in school were unconstitutional. The summer also saw the most famous civil rights march on Washington, when 200,000 turned up to hear Martin Luther King's "I have a dream" speech. Late that fall, about a month after Berry was released, President Kennedy was assassinated while in a motorcade procession through Dallas.

After that event the decade worsened by fits and starts of sporadic violence. The only balance was the heightened freedom brought first by the beat poets of the late fifties and early sixties and then the hippie movement of the late sixties – early seventies.

On the music scene, however, Chuck hadn't missed much. But with Chuck, Elvis, Little Richard, Jerry Lee and Buddy out of the picture, Fats Domino was virtually the only original rock & roller who continued to record. In spite of the absence of the best and brightest pop and rock continued to sell, showing the absurdity of the payola investigations and a rather strange offshoot of pop culture had filled the gap. Scores of white teen idols vied for Elvis' place in the hearts of bobby soxers across the land. It all seemed to converge in Philadelphia, a telling factor in the movement's development.

Dick Clark, a local DJ, had taken over a television program for Bob Horn after Horn was arrested on a charge of drunken driving while his station was holding a campaign to rid the state of inebriated drivers. Philadelphia is a sort of dream test market, and its tough south side provided a wealth of kids who'd long known their only way off the streets would be by becoming either boxers or entertainers.

A whole phalanx of them came from an Italian neighborhood consisting of a few city blocks, and many of them played together when they were kids. In the mid-fifties, Fabian, Bobby Rudell, James Darren and Frankie Avalon would do what Mario Lanza, Eddie Fisher, Al Martino and Buddy Greco (also from the south side) had done for their parents' generation.

These idols were quintessentially late 50s. They seemed to go with the architecture and interior design they call up the kind of graphics Devo might use on an album cover. Many of them were "invented" by the entrepreneurs who caught on to all the marketing aspects of rock & roll that had nothing to do with an ability to write or sing. Fabian was plucked off the street for just such a purpose when his manager saw that Elvis and Ricky Nelson had too many fans who couldn't begin to get close enough.

Their music certainly had more in common with Lanza, et. al. than the rough rhythms of Chuck or Presley's Sun days. In a Bandstand appearance featuring Frankie Avalon's "Venus," the camera panned across a bevy of winsome beauties, dressed in the latest "ballerina" length ball gowns, ensconced by yards of tulle and nylon net. The girls held poses of Grecian beauty on pedestals surrounded by columns. The cameras drew back to reveal Frankie lip-synching the opening lines: "Oh Venus . . ." Taken out of context, the songs seem the height of kitsch, but when lumped with the rest of the 50s trappings – rolled down bobby sox, peter pan collars and wool sweaters (even if you lived in California), penny loafers and barettes – one recognizes the songs as a way of life. With their swooped-back hair dripping with lanolin, these singers' styles mirrored the high tackiness of the fins on a '57 Ford, or, for that matter, the "modern" streamlining that is the automatic stamp of anything made in the 50s. There's something of a Jetsons look to a 50s household, and like much of the furniture in the living room, the songs had the highest of ambitions, often with the most ridiculous results. In 1960, Frankie Avalon sang a tune he detested, "De-De-Dinah," while holding his nose. It sold a million copies.

Berry's "Together (We Will Always Be)"

was one bow he made to schlock rock, with Berry crooning "ex-pecially . . . to you . . ." it sounds as though he was trying to emulate Nat King Cole, but the style just wasn't his forte.

This pseudo-operatic delivery lasted to the very early sixties, maintaining a modicum of excitement, with style if not substance. But soon another phase took over, and in some ways it came about as a branch of the Philly sound.

Frankie and Fabian and the rest had found a new outlet for their waning popularity by appearing in dozens of innocuous movies that centered around the burgeoning California surf-bum scene. In 1961, the Beach Boys and Jan and Dean had finally injected some new influence into the charts. Amazingly enough, the rest of the land-locked nation pounced on the songs, made irresistible not only by the perfectly honed harmonies, but by a beat Chuck Berry had already proven to be undeniably danceable. The Beach Boys' first hit, "Surfin' USA" in 1963 was simply "Sweet Little 16" with new words. It's not hard to imagine how Berry felt when he first heard his rewritten tune while sitting in his jail cell.

Despite the general bankruptcy of the American pop scene in the years Berry was still in jail, there were a number of originals who managed to establish and maintain a voice in the charts. In 1961 Del Shannon released his classic, "Runaway." Roy Orbison emerged as a bankable item with "Running Scared." And Gary U.S. Bonds, who would some 20 years later be unearthed by Bruce Springsteen, released "Quarter to Three," and two tunes from a decidely Berry theme, "School is out," and "School Is In". The following year saw the Sirelles' "Will you Still Love Me Tomorrow?" (written by Carole King) and Little Eva's "Loco-motion." Fats Domino continued pressing out the hits with "You Win Again" released in February of that year, and Berry's hero, Nat King Cole, scored again with "Ramblin' Rose" (a tune Berry would later record) in August. Another odd strain had developed that had its peak during these three years with Frankie Valli and the Four Seasons and Lou Christie, both of whom issued songs featuring a high falsetto lead. The Four Seasons' "Rag Doll" and Christie's "Two Faces Have I" were big hits in these years.

But by late '63 Berry was out of jail and, in an odd reversal of circumstances, industry magazines gleefully anticipated his comeback. As usual it was the British press who realized what effect his release might have, especially as the Mersey beat that was blossoming before their eyes was doing very well recycling the hits of Berry, Little Richard and others.

In June, the English trade magazine *Melody Maker* featured a huge headline with Berry's picture: "DUE FOR TOUR IN AUTUMN." The tour failed to materialize, but his presence on the charts convinced people that some Great Event was coming. Buddy Holly's version of "Brown-Eyed Handsome Man" had resurfaced at #22 on the

English charts, Bo Diddley's "Bo Diddley" made a comeback, and Sheffield singer Dave Grundy changed his name to "Dave Berry" and made some ripples with "Memphis, Tennessee" until Chuck's original was reissued and knocked it off the charts.

In the weeks following, *Melody Maker* supplied bits and pieces of information to keep its readers informed of Berry's latest doings. When Pye, Chess' English label, issued a new single by Berry, "Go Go Go," it shot into the charts in late July. It was proof, *Melody Maker* crowed, that even after five years off the charts "you can't keep a good man down. R & B in general and the big beat in particular have a bigger grip than ever before."

When *Melody Maker* writer Chris Roberts phoned Berry in October at his home in Wentzville, "Memphis" was number 26 and climbing.

Roberts' interview with Berry would be the only time he would speak freely and without rancor about the time he spent in jail. Indeed, his responses were often flecked with humor, even about the term in jail, and Roberts commented on his subject's seeming composure and placidity.

His interests then were home and his business dealings at Berry Park, which were, he said, his "livelihood," taking up half his career. Besides the few benefits he'd done locally, he'd done no professional dates, but, as the earlier article had said, was trying to line up a British tour with the original members of the Chuck Berry Trio – Johnny Johnson and Ebby Harding – who had continued (and still do) gigging in and around St. Louis. In the meantime he was content to stay at home with his wife and four children. (However, his marriage was shattered by his prison sentence, and he would be divorced within two years of his release.)

Roberts asked him if, in 1960, he thought his professional life was over. Berry answered "I never thought it was the end for me three years ago. I have never thought it. One's ambition must be dead to think that, and mine never was.

"I had a programme for myself all worked out, one of the things being a study of music. In fact, I ran out of time for it, which wasn't a bad thing considering the location."

Berry's vitality hadn't been dimmed at all, and he revealed that he had, indeed, spent much of his time working on new material. Which he said was his "major pastime." All the time he'd spent by himself, he said, was a positive factor which "definitely" allowed him to be more creative. But while he maintained that his style had remained unchanged, his playing had taken on a more "adult" approach. "Ray Charles, I have noticed, has done the same thing," said Berry. "But he will always be Ray. Regardless of the mechanics of his playing, he will still have the same style, the same feeling, forever. I would like to think that I have the same approach."

Berry insisted throughout the article that the experience had not been too hard on him,

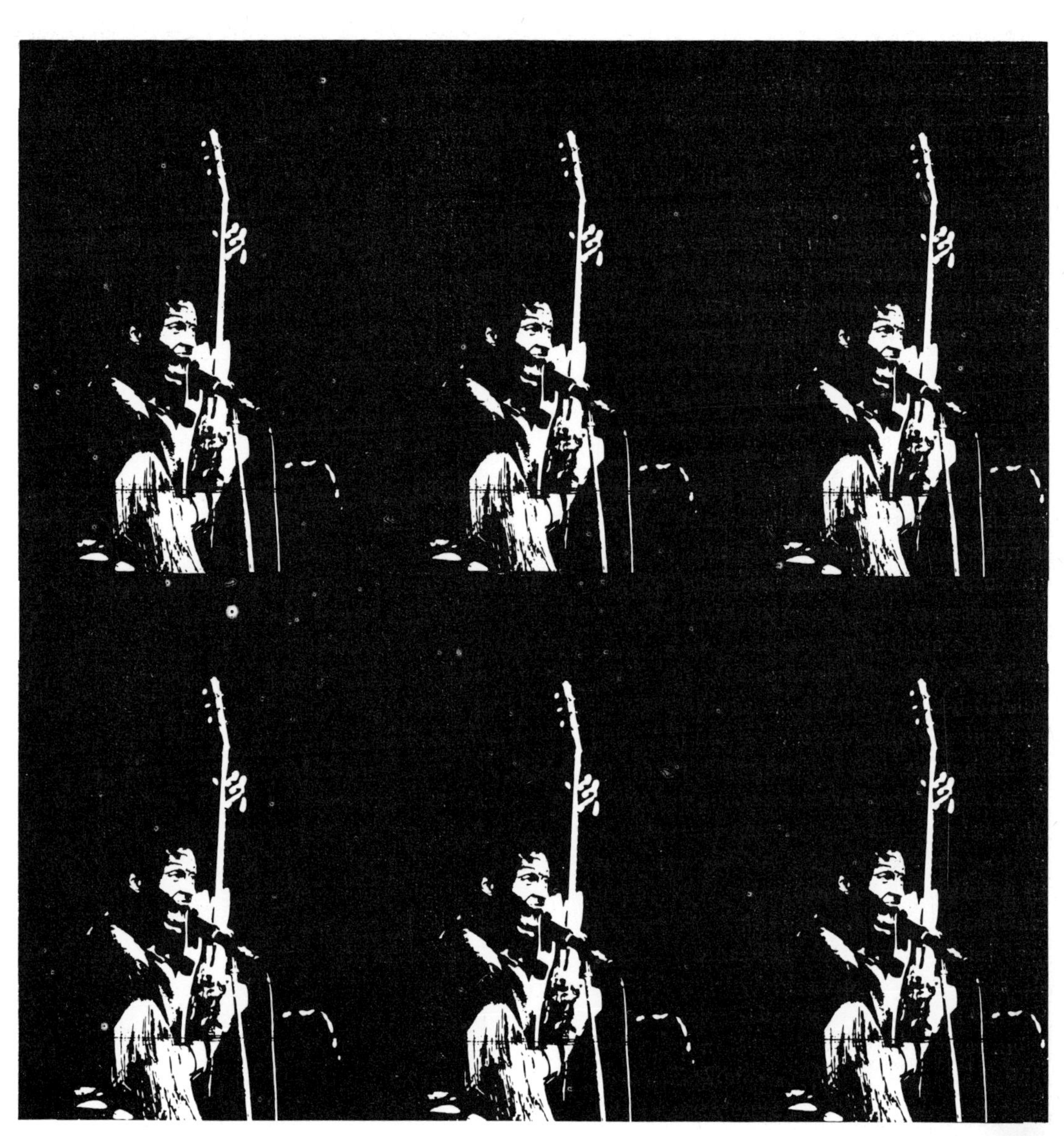

at one point comparing the prison regime to Army life. His solitude had allowed him, he said, to "reach the soul" of what he was trying to do. "I think soul is the only word to describe it – the real bottom of it, the real – you know? It flowed, that's it."

In spite of the fact that Berry would encounter unaccustomed critical scrutiny in the coming years, he would produce some great songs from his years of solitude. Four singles he released in 1964 are as sturdy rockers as anything done before he went in. The first of these, released in February, was "Nadine," which Berry said he purposely patterned after that other bustin' loose number, "Maybellene." There was the same basic scenario involving a chase over hill and dale after the heroine, and in spite of the life Berry might have grown accustomed to on the outside, his heroine sits, in the opening lines, on the city bus. The song soon picks up to "Maybellene"'s motorvating pace, with Berry as a "mounted cavalier" who comandeers a taxi and goes after her "campaign shouting like a Southern diplomat."

The next release, in April, was "No Particular Place to Go," a shuffling hearkening back to basic R & B, which became a top ten hit on both sides of the Atlantic. It was followed by "You Never Can Tell," a real gem packed with the kind of detail one had come to expect from this first poet of rock & roll, down to the couple's TV dinner and ginger-ale-packed fridge. The song was the story of two rock & rollers who married, and Berry left the conclusion up to the listener while bringing up a few questions about whether they actually lived happily ever after. "They bought a souped-up Jidney, it was a cherry red '53," the song goes. They played their "seven hundred little records," blasting their hi-fi phono.

"But when the sun went down, the rapid tempo of the music fell
'C'est la vie,' say the old folks,
'It goes to show you never can tell.' "

Country singer Emmylou Harris recorded the tune on her *Luxury Liner* LP in 1978.

As writers Jeremy Pascall and Rob Burt said, "In 1964, Chuck Berry was not only at the height of his influence, but also at an imaginative peak as a lyricist."

And it was true that he was at the peak of his influence, because by 1964, Beatlemania had begun to grip the entire world. With them, they brought the Rolling Stones and a whole crew of Mersey-beaters to our collective consciousness.

"Roll Over Beethoven" was a regular show-opener for the Beatles, and they put it on their second album and "Rock & Roll Music" went on their third. "Too Much Monkey Business" was another regular part of their stage act. Other groups followed their lead, including the number two Mersey beat group, Gerry and the Pacemakers with "Maybellene," and later, the Kinks, who offered "Beautiful Delilah."

The Rolling Stones, however, arguably were the most indebted to Berry. Keith

Richards and Mick Jagger, who'd known each other in school, reportedly began their friendship in earnest when Richards spotted Jagger in a tube station with a stack of albums under his arm. "Oh, are you into Chuck Berry too?" were the words that cemented their cameraderie. Richards has always played the standard Berry riff, as is very apparent on their early albums. "Carol," "Come On," and Berry's arrangement of "Route 66" appeared on their first album, *The Rolling Stones*, issued in May of '64. The second album, *12 X 5*, featured "Around and Around," and "Bye Bye Johnny," as well as "Confessin' the Blues," the song Berry sang at his first public appearance while he was still in high school. On the same LP, (which includes the classic "Time Is on My Side") is "2120 S. Michigan Ave." the old Chess address. "Route 66" appears again on *December's Children* ('65); "Around and Around" resurfaced on *Love You Live* ('77). *Get Yer Ya Yas Out* (1970) offered both "Carol" and "Little Queenie." These last two had become highlights of their live act, along with their inimitable version of "Johnny B. Goode."

But just as important as the actual songs they borrowed from Berry was the spirit that imbued their music. They had heard it like anyone else, though perhaps a heightened element of suppression appealed to a greatly developed sense of drama. Their wholesale acceptance of what was by then ten-year-old music injected a new vigor into the languid rock scene.

It was a cycle that would be repeated again and again, with artists from the US gaining acceptance in England they never found at home, the British taking the music as their own and translating it to a movement that returned across the Atlantic and took the country by storm. Artists as diverse as Bill Haley, Berry, Jimi Hendrix, the Ramones, Television and Lou Reed would prompt such syndromes.

Even as the Quarrymen, John Lennon and Paul McCartney's skiffle group, the Beatles had included Chuck Berry and Little Richard numbers as part of their repertoire. Berry stories abound as part of their early days: Cindy and Dot (John and Paul's girlfriends) spending many long afternoons playing Little Richard and Chuck Berry 45s over and over again so they could transcribe the words; Pete Best's bass drum rolling across the stage once they started on a Berry song; the first strains of "Roll Over Beethoven" undoing their carefully stacked pompadours; and from Berry himself, the wunderkind Beatles at the height of their fame staring at him in wide-eyed amazement as he performed in London in 1966. (Berry seemed a bit bewildered by all the fuss about the Beatles. In subsequent interviews, he always said be liked the Everley Brothers better.)

The effect of the Beatles and the Rolling Stones was far-reaching. For the first time, Melody Maker reported English records at the top of their charts in 1963. The trend would take over in the US as well. In the next

TRIUMPH
TRIUMPH
TRIUMPH

A scene from *American Graffiti*

few years, the English Invasion would prove just how wrong the record companies were in their predictions that the music was just another phase, somewhat akin to acne, that kids would grow out of once they passed their oily pubescence. At the height of surfdom and schlock rock, record sales in pop music had grown from 20% of the dollar volume of all sales in 1956 to 45%. In the single year following (63–64), the English invasion brought the total to 60%, and the percentage would continue to climb through heavy metal and glitter rock to a total of about 80% by 1975. Each year, the market was rejuvenated – and more often than not, a rock & roller, once he'd had a taste of the forbidden fruit, didn't return to Frank or Perry or whatever adult songster was then the rage.

The charts took on a different character altogether. Gold records (1,000,000 sold) in years past had been scarce items, with none at all issued in 1960, and two or three in the years following. In 1964, however, the Beatles were the recipients of three of the seven issued. In 1965, they were joined by Petula Clark, Herman's Hermits, and the Rolling Stones. Twenty-four gold records were issued the following year, and the list (now heterogeneous) lengthens thereafter.

As far as lyrics went, the influences the English beat brought were too numerous to count. Just now, reverberations of that second wave still echo in the Beatle-y harmonies of the Go-Go's.

The Beatles also revolutionized rock cinema with the release of "A Hard Day's Night," far more intelligent than the endless beach movies and Elvis melodramas of years past. It would make way for a new group of "better" rock movies with varying degrees of plot. Chuck was in another film released that year that also broke new ground. Released under "The T.A.M.I. Show" and retitled "Teenage Command Performance" before settling on "Gather No Moss," the movie documented a stand-out collection of artists, both old and new. It was one of the first to capture a live performance at the Santa Monica Civic Auditorium. Jan and Dean opened the move in skateboards, lip-synching "From All Over the World" to introduce the various groups, including the Rolling Stones, the Beach Boys, the Bararians, Chuck, James Brown and his Fabulous Flames, Marvin Gaye, Gerry and the Pacemakers, Lesley Gore, Jan and Dean, Billy J. Kramer and the Dakotas, the Supremes, and Smokey Robinson and the Miracles. Despite a hammy Chuck, who seemed to get a real rise out of waving to the audience, the performances were sell-served by the immediacy lent by newly-developed hand-held equipment. Advances in film labs, as well, had made the technique possible, and it would be the basis for the hugely successful *Woodstock* and the documentary of the horrors at Altamount, *Gimme Shelter*.

By 1966, Berry felt strong enough to consider other labels to record his new material. Leaving Chess would be a wrenching decision. He'd seen many changes in the last ten years, and the Chesses were more to him than executives. But in the end, he chose to go to Mercury for a $150,000 advance. When he told Leonard Chess his decision, Chess responded, "Go, and you'll be back in three years".

30 January 1981. (Left) Chuck is presented with a Distinguished Merit Award by Mary Crosby. (Above) With Latoya and Michael Jackson

After the release of *Concerto in B. Goode*, Berry fulfilled Leonard Chess' prophecy and returned to the studios at 2120 S. Michigan Ave. There was much speculation on why Berry returned to Chess when he did. Critical appraisal of the Mercury albums varied, with American critics moaning at the loss of the original, immediate sound; on the other hand, the editors of England's New Musical Express declared the albums some of his best when considered as a whole, *Sergeant Pepper*-style. But it's less than likely that Berry paid much attention to the critics. Chess was home in a way that Mercury was not, and it was geographically closer to his farm in Wentzville. Leonard Chess had died, but his son Marshal had taken over, and Phil remained as well. They knew him and were used to his moods and knew the importance of keeping the relationship healthy by insuring a good cash flow. One story that made the industry rounds may be apocryphal, but seems characteristic of Berry the businessman. Berry had startled the Mercury staff by dropping in and demanding money for one of the albums recently released. When an aide tried to explain the system of royalty statements that were released every six months, he became more impatient. An alert executive told the aide to issue a check, but that wasn't what Berry had in mind either. The Chesses, on the other hand, were more used to dealing in cash. When Phil bought Chicago's leading soul station, WVON in 1963, he paid cash – $1 million in $10,000 bills.

Not long after Berry returned, Phil sold

the company to the giant GRT tape corporation for an estimated $10 million. The two remaining Chesses stayed on for a while, but Phil died in '74 and Marshal took on responsibilities with Rolling Stones Records in the early 70s.

The transaction was the end of an era, and it was ironic that Berry chose to return at this point because he had represented the label's peak after many years of recording a phlanx of R&B stars.

Still Berry was able to charge an auditorium with excitement, as he did in the same year as his return to Chess with a visit to London's Albert Hall, headlining for the Who.

Times were changing, all right. He was now 43 and psychedelia was blossoming. For a year, the San Francisco sound had occupied the consciousness of the Bay Area and it was seeping inland. Jefferson Airplane, the Grateful Dead, the Doors and the Who were manifestations of R&B no one had yet imagined. In spite of each of these groups' trademark sounds, like the Doors' carnivalesque organ and shaman lead singer, the Dead's luded-out delivery or the Airplane's only slightly controlled mania, there was something that bound them together besides drugs – their lyrics, which addressed kids directly and of course that regular chonka-chonka-chonka guitar. And as John Lennon said, anything that went chonka-chonka-chonka was Chuck Berry.

A man who'd been playing on the East and West Coasts since the 50s with the Isley Brothers had begun his own act but was literally starving. Chas Chandler of the Animals advised him to put together a flashy act and go to England. English fans once again showed the savvy Americans lacked and sent him home a star. The Jimi Hendrix Experience was born.

Hendrix was the epitome – and final act of – Woodstock. Like the others of the Bay Area who would die young (Joplin, Morrison), he would be idolized as the spokesman for a generation. Many thought of him as Berry's latest interpreter – he owed much to Berry for the flashy guitar tricks, such as playing behind his back and with his teeth, and, like Berry he was less a "black performer" than someone at the forefront of a primarily white movement, and better at it than most.

Though the Who, who were kicking up a lot of interest in old-style rock & roll, were representative of the late 60s revival of interest, one by one the older stars were fading out. By 1969, of the stars still living, Bill Haley, Berry, Bo Diddley and Jerry Lee Lewis had begun to cede from the average kid's consciousness. Probably Berry was the most tenacious of the lot, but in July of '69 he played at New York's Pavilion to an audience of 600 in an auditorium that held 6,000.

Enter Richard Nader, a former agent who, with no money in his pocket, rented out Madison Square Garden with the idea of holding a revival concert. He then set about looking up the ones he had in mind, and first on the list was Bill Haley. Haley had lived in Mexico for the last few years, and hadn't

played in the U.S. for the past eight, although he had toured some in South America. Nader spent about 30 hours over the span of the next few weeks on the phone to Mexico convincing Haley he was serious and working out details. For the rest of his roster, he wanted his personal favorite, the Platters, whose first hit was "Smoke Gets in Your Eyes," but are known better for their version of "The Great Pretender." The Shirelles and the Coasters nearly completed the bill, but Nader knew he needed another big draw, so he called Berry's agent in L.A. Nader made the date with the agent, but when later phone calls failed to convince him of Nader's ability to pay, the agent booked Berry in a New Hampshire college, a fact Nader discovered after he had printed flyers advertising Berry. The promoter showed up at the agent's office, this time with money he'd finally received from a sponsor. "I offered him $250 more," says Nader. "I offered the agent $250 to lose the contract. I bought [the agent] a hi-fi." In total, he paid $2250 for that first concert in fees to Berry. That left the relatively small problem of talking the college into changing the date of their concert (their homecoming). They did and Berry appeared as scheduled. Nader's concert was a success and he has since made it an annual event, with headliners Bo Diddley, Jerry Lee Lewis, Fats Domino, Lesley Gore, Lou Christie and the like.

Nader confirms other reports of Berry's off-stage moodiness and generally strange behaviour. "From the first, he created problems," said Nader. Berry was unhappy with the shared top billing with the Platters, didn't want to play two shows, and was "very upset" when Nader had the Platters close the first. Bill Haley, on the other hand, was "glad to get the money," in Nader's opinion. Berry does demand cash before he plays, which he counts in the presence of the promoter, and he insists that two Dual Showman reverb amps be provided for his performances. Nader claims he has also, minutes before a concert was to begin, demanded more cash than was agreed on, and that he refuses to sign contracts or receipts. Often, says Nader, Berry will leave his guitar in the car until he's been paid.

All this is perhaps understandable coming from a man who had a quarter of the writing rights to his first, biggest hit taken away from him "in lieu of my rookiness" as he put it. But Nader claims that in the 12 years he's known him, Berry has put him through some harrowing times.

"At times, I thought I was getting close to him," he said. But at a Pittsburgh concert, Berry demanded more money before the show and when Nader wouldn't deliver, Berry went onstage and spent 45 minutes "tuning up." Finally Berry said, "I want the promoter to come out here," and told the crowd Nader hadn't paid him. Nader, furious, refused to come out, saying, "Just fucking *play*, Chuck." Eventually the audience started booing and Berry went on with the show.

Nader also reports that for the making of the movie *Let the Good Times Roll*, which

used segments of his first concert, he sent a film crew out to Wantzville to film Berry on his farm.

Director Sid Levin, who was responsible for this excellent rock film, confirms Nader's reports of Berry's unpredictable behaviour. Levin called Berry from LA a week or so before they were to begin shooting, and Berry agreed to spend a few days with the filmmaker so they could get to know each other.

They went together to a concert where Berry was performing in Salem, Oregon. Whey they got there, Levin remembers, the crowd was "boisterous, demanding Chuck Berry." Meanwhile, Berry, his blond girlfriend and Levin went backstage to the manager's office. There the manager gave Berry his cash. The image of Berry counting his money stuck with Levin. "He looked like some kind of card shark, he was counting it out so fast," said Levin. Then Berry put the money in his attache case ("I felt like we were pulling off a heist," said Levin) and straightened. "This is short," Berry said. The manager was flustered; he insisted it *was* the amount they'd agreed on. Berry asked Levin to hold the attache case backstage for him while he went onstage.

"The crowd finally had him," said Levin. "They screamed loudly. Then Chuck plays one or two notes and unplugs his guitar. 'What the hell is going on?' says the manager. 'These are not the amplifiers I asked for,' says Chuck." The two went backstage again while the manager coughed up a few more bucks.

After the show, Berry, Levin and the blond went to a Chinese restaurant and then back on the road towards Portland. A few miles out, they had a flat. They fixed it and went on, only to have another a little farther down the road. Finally they figured out that the kind people in Salem had slashed the tires. "I thought, 'OK, now I'm going to spend the night in the woods with the guy who wrote "Maybellene," " said Levin.

The few days he'd spent with Berry on the road were good, said Levin, and Berry seemed "very warm." But there was a subtle change when Levin flew to St Louis to meet him there. Berry was an hour late in getting to the airport, and seemed a bit distant, but he soon warmed again and gave Levin a tour of the town, including the mansion he shared with his wife and the house he'd grown up in.

Then they drove to Berry Farm, which was enclosed by an electric wire fence. Levin met the staff, among whom was a young anorectic-looking blond whom he was sure was a groupie. While Levin was on the upper floors of the main building, Berry went down to greet a guest who'd come in from New York. As Levin looked down from the windows above, he saw "these two black men (Berry and his visitor), both over six feet, followed by this emaciated, anemic young thing carrying the suitcases."

Berry showed Levin the rest of the farm, including the guitar-shaped swimming pool and the recording and video equipment. But the following day, when they were to shoot, Berry met him wearing sunglasses and he was "*uptight*, and I mean uptight, acting real different. I asked him, 'What's wrong, Chuck?

I want you to be comfortable.'" Berry responded with a terse "I feel fine."

They then shot the sequences around Berry's bus, with which Levin was enormously pleased. "He was theatrical in a subtle way," said Levin, and didn't communicate any of the uneasiness to the camera that Levin had seen so obviously a few minutes before.

While Levin and his crew stayed on Berry's compound (which Levin described as a group of clean but rather cheap and tawdry pasteboard buildings), the cameraman had to be taken to the doctor to treat a redwood splinter that had lodged in his eye. The assistant cameraman drove him there and they returned shaken, saying Berry had met them at the gate with a rifle. Levin believes their story, saying, "One of them had been everywhere and didn't scare easily. He was sure he was looking at death."

A few days before, Berry had described to Levin the manner in which he had left one small southern town. As he drove out, one of the local authorities stopped him, walked over to the car, put his big palm on Berry's windshield and leaned in. "If you ever come back, I'll kill you," (or words to that effect) was his final farewell to that town. When Levin and his film crew left the Berry compound, Berry met them at the gate and replayed that bizarre episode, this time with Berry in the role of the local authority.

The thoughts Levin were left with were "mainly what a bizarre, sad, compulsive place he was in ..." He also left with a very different idea of why people are the way they are. "It's like a pendulum that swings between freedom and compulsion," he said.

If the portrayal seems a bit paranoic, Nader has more: he claims Berry owns land in Toronto, and has worked out an "escape route" directly there that would take him even if bus and rail lines were down. "Of all the artists in rock & roll, he is one of the three – Elvis, Paul Anka and Chuck – who has held onto his money." Nader cited holdings in real estate, publishing and the recording industry.

"You use my name," Nader says Berry told him: "You take money from the public. I show up. You pay me."

It seems that his paranoia manifested itself even more greatly in the late 60s and early 70s than it had in the time immediately following his release from jail when Carl Perkins had commented on his change in attitude. In '68, he chased a Ramparts reporter from his grounds in Wentzville after giving tentative agreement to an interview. In '72, in a rare interview with William Patrick Salvo, he denied he'd ever gone to jail at all and told the reporter to "look it up in the local papers." Salvo did and found the conviction reported. It was in this interview that Salvo brought up the subject of a concert at the L.A. Palladium where Keith Richards jumped onstage to jam and played (as is his habit) very loudly. Berry kicked him off. He told Salvo he didn't recognize Richards; all he knew was that he "couldn't be heard" against the guitar and piano (Dr. John) that seemed to get louder with each song. "Gee, I love the cat," said Berry. "... I guess it was just a bad night; they

must have been high or something." The blurb on Salvo in that *Rolling Stone* issue said he was then working on Berry's biography (which never appeared).

At around this same time, Berry began bringing his daughter Ingrid onstage. At 28, she was a beautiful young carbon copy of her father and provided backup vocals.

In 1972, Berry had his very first number one record after 17 years in the business with the innocuous ditty "My Ding-A-Ling." The album for which it was released, *The London Chuck Berry Sessions*, also went high on the charts. The single had appeared in somewhat different form as "My Tambourine" on the 1958 release *Berry's on Top*. Some remember the song as uncannily familiar to "My Toy Bell" by the Bees (1954). "Let's just say I might have heard it," Berry told an interviewer about "Toy Bell."

Some avid Berry fans were actually incensed at the sound of the record, which had none of the driving rhythm of his earlier releases. But in spite of the fact that some were sure that "My Ding-A-Ling" was proof that Berry was going soft, Mercury product manager Johnny Sippel told Salvo, " "Ding-A-Ling" is something I'm sure he wrote 20 years ago . . . as I remember both Mr Greene (Irving B. Greene, Mercury's president) and myself threw that thing out . . . "

The song catches Berry when he is enjoying himself most, and that seems to be whenever he can lead an audience into some kind of organized chaos. In these later years, Berry had honed concerts down to a craft, and the best ones were those in which he had a real interplay with the audience. "You say 'em, we play 'em" has been the rule for the last 20 odd years, and most shows end when he brings 10 or so from the audience up to dance as he makes his exit. Berry seems to have fixed on the atmosphere of a classroom from his earliest songs like "School Days," and it's that atmosphere that prevails at his best concerts. Berry carefully instructs the audience on its part, chiding them for coming in too soon or too late with all the seriousness of a schoolmarm. His final goal seems to be to inject a good dose of licentiousness or at least vivaciousness into the crowd, something that was tactily forbidden in his heyday. He seems to like playing games with them, and of course the audience likes whatever he likes. Even promoter Nader admits that in spite of the problems he's encountered offstage with Berry, the man "never delivered less than 110% on the stage . . . never left until the last person was standing."

To promote "Ding-A-Ling" and the album, Berry went on an extensive tour of the U.S. and Britain and played in London to what newspapers reported as an "unprecedented response." As ever, it was the English fans who first acknowledged it – Berry was back.

In March of that year he'd had a less jovial response at his Las Vegas debut. His old nemesis Elvis Presley was packing them in with a super-glitzy show at the Aladdin Hotel, and to many the show was a pitiful spectacle, but fans turned up in droves. Wearing an Evel-Kneival styled jumpsuit and grossly over-

weight, Presley made his entrance to the overture from *2001: A Space Odyssey*, played by a full orchestra with a huge brass section. While he was packing them in the main showroom, Berry was slated for the lounge.

Las Vegas could hardly be considered the best place for Chuck Berry – he was rough and ragged where the rest was glitz and schmaltz. One could hardly imagine the average Las Vegas audience jumping up and down on their chairs to "Memphis, Tennessee" either. Berry proved to be a tough act offstage, as usual, reportedly upping his price for the second night and demanding the two Dual amps, as usual. Which had to be flown in from California. He has yet to return there, which might have been no great loss for him.

His next acts were better – in December, he visited New York's Villageast, and the following month, he and Jerry Lee Lewis brought down the house at that ol' fellowship hall called Carnegie. Patricia Haire, *Daily News* critic, lamented at the rows of empty seats and called it "one of the best shows of its kind seen in these parts in quite a while." Although Jerry Lee was forced to open for him once again, this time maybe the rather uptown atmosphere caused him to refrain from the pyrotechnics. Haire said of Berry's performance: "... the audience screamed and stomped and danced and waved their arms until it looked like some sort of surrealistic revival meeting."

In 1973, Berry would appear in yet another movie called *London Rock & Roll*, which gave backstage glimpses of the performers Chuck, Little Richard, Bill Haley and Jerry Lee Lewis. A crowd of true fanatics turned up in pompadours and sideburns, stovepipe pants, white socks and black crepe-soled shoes. Many had come dressed in Ted gear, with long Edwardian-style coats; there were rockers too in black leather. Several denim jackets bore the names "Eddie Cochran-Gene Vincent" on the back.

Haley braved the crowd before the others and gave the people what they wanted. After sliding through "Crazy Man Crazy" and "See Ya Later, Alligator," he had to play "Rock Around the Clock" twice because nothing would top it.

The Killer was next, and with his usual panache set the place on its ear. He did all the good old stuff: kicked the stool away from the piano, got his wavy hair all down in his eyes, stared at the audience with a glint of dementia in his eyes and started with just one finger twirling: "You can shake it one time for me, can't ya?" Then he busted loose and started the grind and bump, standing on his baby grand. "SHAKE, BABY, SHAKE ..."

Haley had been introduced as "the King," Jerry Lee as "the Killer," and as soon as Little Richard bounded onstage he proclaimed loudly, "*I'm* the King! *I'm* the King!" and attacked the piano for "Lucille." Before he finished the first song, he was dripping with sweat and dove into "Tutti Frutti" with even more abandon. Dressed in the skin-tight bright yellow leotard-like suit Mick Jagger would

adopt for later tours, his pencil-thin moustache brimming his upper lip, curls spilling over a headband, he jumped into the crowd, deftly avoiding grabbing hands, but simply bouncing around until the front rows were hopping, too. By the time he left the stage, the audience was packed to the front, sweating, moving and gyrating.

Then Chuck came out, dressed in the clothes he had adopted for the psychedelic era: bright red trousers and paisley shirt, with long sideburns, nearly to the jawbone. One by one, he went through the catalog: "Carol," "Memphis," "Brown-Eyed Handsome Man," "No Particular Place to Go." When he asked for requests, the crowd was ready: "Na-DINE!" "Reelin' & Rockin" and of course "Maybellene."

London Rock & Roll shows some of the best footage ever of Berry: He is relaxed and his movements seems totally without strain. At one point, as he's going down in the splits, long legs wide apart and the guitar nearly touching the floor, swaying this way and that, he looks directly into the camera at the edge of the stage. His face takes up most of the screen for a minute looking as if he's daring the cameraman to catch him offguard for even a second, and shaking his head lightly as if he's telling a funny story. All the while he's picking the notes like mad and missing none.

Berry's hot in this show, so it was more than startling when sudden silence descended in the middle of a duck-walk through "Johnny B. Goode." Some kind of power failure had cut off the guitars and mikes at the height of his act. Backstage with the film crew, he compared the incident to coitus interruptus. "There I was without my climax . . . you know what being without your climax is like. We finally got the problem fixed and went back out . . ." And so he did, taking the act to its natural conclusion.

The rest of '75 was a good year for him – he showed again at Richard Nader's sixth anniversary show and toured England to the same appreciative audiences, opening at the Odeon in Lewisham, southeast London once the center of old-style rock & roll. A poll of DJs and critics for the Rock Music Awards placed him in the Don Kirschner Hall of Fame.

In '76 another swing took him back through the UK, appearing at places like the Palais Lido, Douglas, Isle of Man.

The only release of this period, on Chess, is *Bio*, and the cover photos alone are worth the price of the LP for the avid Berry fan. A mischievous Chuck at about 12 years old in front of some billboards and an old grocery store peers out at you, and the inside shows a younger Chuck below a picture of Abraham Lincoln. Another is one that has all the signs of having been shot in a Woolworth's photo booth when he was about 14. Yet another looks like a senior high school portrait, with a patently exuberant Berry, another shows him playing at a party or small club surrounded by dancing black couples, and at the bottom there's a shot of the arty Berry, wearing a

black beret with the neck of his Gibson sticking up in the corner. A couple of the shots are with Alan Freed, presumably during the making of *Rock Rock Rock*, another shows him with Johnny Johnson and Ebby Harding. On the right there's a picture of his tour bus above a shot of Berry accepting a gold record award with Richard Nader at his side.

The album is a bit uneven, but its name is appropriate, because the themes keep coming back to hearth and home, on which Berry places so much importance. The music almost seems a hearkening back to pre-rock days in many respects. A couple of the tunes are very bluesy, like "Aimlessly Drifting" and "Hello Little Girl Goodbye" and the title track, "Bio." The album must be something of what he'd had in mind when he approached Leonard Chess about cutting a blues album under a pseudonym years ago.

Two of the songs, "Bio" and "Got It and Gone," are slowed-down versions of "Johnny B. Goode." In "Bio" he begins in St Louis, where his mama was working "just to keep us six kids alive." From there, it's a much more literal version of his life story than "Goode" told, this time, in the first person. The trip to Chicago to meet Muddy Waters, the first song that "jumped on the charts" and the journey to Hollywood are all recounted. The song ends like most of his shows, with Berry talking about how he loves to play and bring "many happy hours" and that it's the only thing he's learned how to do.

"Get It and Gone" is another sort of musical bio. It starts with the first song a singer learns to play and takes him through the time he spends in the Army. On landing at Clark Air Force Base after his release, he gives a free show for everyone on the street.

Of the rest of the songs, there's a very country "Rain Eyes," the instrumental "Woodpecker" and "Talkin' to My Buddy," a shuffling R&B number about the search for the one true love with a girl who may just be a bit too young.

The album's easy amiability makes it a pleasure after many plays; there's a sense of respite after long, hard work. And there's the same charm of the lyrics: these are simple amusements, and many of the songs are sad little stories with a last-line happy ending. "Rain Eyes" in particular may grate the ear at first, but there's something about the harmony that is endearing. Anyone who's heard the harmonizing in a backwoods church will recognize it, likewise anyone who's heard the Carter family sing. The images here have more in common with a Grandma Moses painting than teenage trappings, and they are evidence of graceful aging with no loss of adolescent idealism and naivete. Berry was probably the only pop artist around at the time who could record such an un-selfconscious record. Top pop material it is not, but Berry fans will find much to like.

By 1978, enough time had elapsed to allow the sharp contrasts and tensions of the 50s fade into the soft-edged outlines of nostalgia. "Happy Days," a TV sitcom about the era

began and spun off "Laverne and Shirley," both centering on inhibited white kids trying to get dates. A Columbia release of that year, *American Hot Wax*, recalled Alan Freed's heyday in vaguely reverential awe, following him through an average day discovering doo-wop singers on doorsteps, signing artists in his office and overseeing recording in the studio. Freed is protrayed as a cool, somewhat distanced presence whose monologue over the air is more like the laid-back FM DJ than the manic Freed who turned so many on to rock & roll in those early days.

The Killer and Chuck are there, but when the box office receipts are confiscated by the cops, Freed has to tell them he can't pay. "Well," says Chuck, "I'll do it for rock & roll." He responds with the bawdy version of "Reelin' and Rockin'."

In real life, Berry knew he had already done enough for rock & roll and maintained his businesslike demeanor even from the earliest days. One interviewer asked him if he ever thought of retiring and Berry replied, "I'll play until I get tired or people get tired of listening to me, and I expect the latter will happen first." Promoter Paul Baratta of the Fillmore West told *Ramparts* reporter Michael Lydon this quote from Berry: "See, I'll never play, never *ever* play for less than $1000 a night. So some day I'll get a call from some 22-year-old punk promoter and he'll say he really wants me but he can only offer $950. And I'll tell him, Congratulations, son, you've just become the man who retired the great Chuck Berry."

In June of the following year, Berry came up against the arm of the law that retired Al Capone and lost, but he fared a little better than the gangster. This formidable adversary was not the FBI or Elliot Ness, but an overt agency that sends shrieks of fear and disbelief every spring from homes across the U.S.: the Internal Revenue Service.

He was indicted that June on a charge of failing to report some $110,000 in income earned for a series of 12 concerts in 1973, and the government charged his actions proved the intent to avoid taxes. Berry had reported earning $374,982 that year in a joint return with his wife, Thetita, but among the other concerts in which he earned around $10,000 for each performance was a sudden dip to a figure of $280, or scale musicians' wages, which Berry claimed to have earned. The government charged that Berry ordered false contracts made, took home $45,000 in cash in a suitcase, changed it to cashier's checks and turned them into certificates of deposit in an attempt to hide the source. His insistence on payment of cash and refusal to sign receipts, they said, was further proof of his guilt. Another $45,000 went unreported from a European tour, the government charged. Prosecutor Tim Wilson estimated his taxable earnings at $589,555.

Richard Nader was called to testify, because he was among the promoters who paid Berry in this time, and he corroborated the government's stand. He'd paid Berry between $9,000 and $11,000 for the concerts he'd played in the rock & roll revival shows.

Nader said Berry tried to imply he'd fallen on hard times and Nader was "helping him out" by giving the $280 per show.

In the end, though, Berry pleaded guilty and said Wilson's assessment was "generally correct." He had chosen to be tried by a California court rather than St Louis because he wasn't sure he would get a fair trial in his home state. The memories of his treatment there in 1959-62 were most likely still very much with him.

Berry's attorney, Bruce Hochman, and the government wrangled over the exact amount that remained untaxed, with Hochman claiming $100,000 and the government claiming twice that. Assistant U.S. Attorney Kathleen March urged a stiff sentence, saying he had failed to admit the full amount, and added, "What we have here is calculated activities to avoid paying taxes. This man has $2.6 million of net worth. The motivation was not need. It was greed."

Hochman called the incidents in 1973 "an aberration," pointing out that the government had gone over Berry's records for other years and found nothing wrong. Most cases involve ongoing violations over a number of years, he said.

Before the judge handed down his sentence, Berry made an impassioned plea stressing his ability and desire to meet the terms of a plan his attorney suggested to pay his dues, which called for a suspended three-year sentence and 10 benefit concerts, along with 500 hours of community work to discourage kids from drug abuse. He knew he had a "strong influence" on many members of society, and although some of his fans were older now, he knew he could help by using his talent to discourage their abuse of "drugs and pills."

When he started talking about the effect the news would have on his aged parents, Berry burst into tears. "I am pretty good at holding my own in front of many, many people," he said. "But it's this office here that causes me to choke up a little bit. It's impossible to hide the results of this from my parents . . . I seem to get publicity on all the wrong things." A too-familiar routine may have been called up by the courtroom from years ago, or possibly the thing that brought him close to so many teenagers in the 50s – a natural fear and hatred of authority – betrayed him in the middle of the staid proceedings. "I'm sorry. It shall not happen again," he said.

U.S. District Judge Harry Preger gave him a sentence based on Hochman's suggestion consisting of 120 days in the federal prison at Lompoc, California, benefit concerts and 1,000 hours of community work. Having been advised of Berry's business agreements at his farm and for performances, he gave him 30 days to get his affairs in order and allowed him to make a 12-day European tour before reporting to Lompoc on Aug. 10.

Many of the music writers who reported his conviction and the concerts before his term reacted with shock and cynicism. Ken Tucker of the L.A. *Herald-Examiner* described an early August concert at the Roxy as a "raucous, happily haphazard one" with a smart,

enthusiastic pick-up band that fought for dear life trying to keep up with him. Tucker closed his review with: "At the Roxy, Berry's last song before an encore was one of his most expansive and optimistic, 'Promised Land.' The promised land referred to is, of course, America, a place Chuck Berry has always so gleefully celebrated and is now once again denied to its celebrator."

More than one writer noted that just two months previously, Berry had entertained an audience of over 1,000 including President Carter at the White House as one of the invited performers to help celebrate Black Musicians' Month.

Just before entering Lompoc, Berry agreed to be interviewed by the L.A. *Times'* Robert Hilburn in his agent's office, where he expressed surprise that he was considered newsworthy material. "I can see them putting my picture in the paper if I do a concert or if we take out an ad, but I never felt like a celebrity," he said.

He would use the four months ahead of him to work on his autobiography, which he was "close to bringing out," he told Hilburn. He said when he first caught on to the fact that writers wanted to know about the man as well as the music, "I shamed them. I'd say, if that's what you want to talk about, blah, blah, blah. But now I'm ready to talk about those things."

But all Hilburn really got from Berry was a confirmation of his birthdate (1926) and that the reform school stay and Mann Act conviction were fact, plus a few interesting comments:

"When I read things like, 'He lost his chance for freedom because of the tax problems' or 'The Indian girl robbed him of his career,' they don't bring me down. I don't have the ability to absorb success or fame so I don't have the ability to absorb pain or disgrace . . . if you need one, you're going to have to put up with the other," he said.

Berry listed his early influences (Nat King Cole, Sinatra, June Christy), and when Hilburn asked what songs of the current pop crop he liked, he came up with a rather surprising list of "Yesterday" by the Beatles, the Everlys "Wake Up, Little Suzy" and Joe South's "Down in the Boondocks," as well as Kenny Rogers' "(You Picked a Fine Time to Leave Me) Lucille."

There was a tinge of disappointment in Hilburn's article that Berry, the father of rock, failed to provide a disparaging opinion of disco, which had taken over after the end of psychedelia.

"Disco is just rock with an exaggerated beat and lights, effects, and a few other things. Rock has always been dance music, happy music. That's why it has lasted. People like to be happy."

By the time he had entered the minimum security camp at Lompoc, his Atlantic release, *Rock It*, was on the stands.

Gibson

Just a couple of months after his release from Lompoc Berry would return yet again, unbowed and apparently as strong as ever. At 53, he was just starting his second comeback, both from his second stint in prison and from another period in which his music had become less than fashionable. The horrors of disco and smoothly produced California sounds like the Eagles' were beginning to wane and in England, the swift and nearly complete immersion in the new wave had taken place two years before. He was seeing a second, less dramatic replay of the events of 15 years past. It had been just twelve years before that he'd played with the Steve Miller Band during the hippie days at Bill Graham's Fillmore West.

Rock It, his latest release to date, is a surprisingly good album, although none of the songs received any airplay. Johnny Johnson is back manning the keyboards after *Bio*'s use of Elephant's Memory. "Oh What a Thrill" is an oldstyle rocker; there's a naughty "If I were" and a new, more subtle arrangement of the oldie, "Havana Moon." The album also includes "House Lights," which Berry now uses to close all his shows.

In December, San Francisco's Old Waldorf advertised a "coming out party" which would be Berry's first after the jail term. His daughter, Ingrid, accompanied him and provided backing vocals, as she had in the past, and provided an eerie, almost ghostlike complment. Reedy-thin, like her father, with his same features, it was she who added some points of grace to her father's all-out rocking. Mark Naftalin, of the R & B Revue Band, provided piano backing, and on guitar was Mel Brown, a veteran from Bobby "Blue" Bland's outfit. He played an unheard-of two hours, *with* an encore, and seemed genuinely happy to be back onstage again. Standing in front of a crowd of hard-core fanatics in a black velvet jacket, he elicited from writer Joel Selvin of the *San Francisco Chronicle* the feeling that the man was much more than an old rocker – he was "an emotional symbol" of "the rock & roll outlaw."

An appearance he made in March of '80 was just as emotionally charged. It was his first trip to New York since his release, and as is his habit, he played with a "pick-up" band – local musicians who could give Berry the backing he needed. It was simply taken for granted that they could play the tunes without rehearsal. Such practices lead to uneven performances at best, but this particular gig at the downtown disco Heat went well.

The place was packed, and plagued by a few problems that are only too common in the club circuit. The house had been oversold, and twice the club's capacity turned up to hear Berry. An angry crowd of about a thousand milled around the outside.

Pianist Howie Wyeth found out he'd be playing for one of his idols about two days before the actual gig. His excitement was so great that a year and a half later, he still got breathless talking about it. He remembers clearly the harrowing minutes with the throng out front, which only got worse when someone from inside yelled, "Anybody from the band out here?" and scores of voices answered, "YES! I'M IN THE BAND!" But Wyeth and the rest of the back-up band, including "maniac guitarist" Harold Palladin, Rick Paley on bass, and Greg Keplinger on drums, somehow made it inside and wriggled through the crowd. "They were really up for it," said Wyeth. "The first set went an hour and 20 minutes" – again an unusually long performance for Berry. Fire department officials made an appearance before the second show and some of the tension outside was finally eased. Berry arrived with daughter Ingrid (who didn't sing at this engagement) in "some kind of Buick Skylark" with another woman who formed a kind of protective ring around him. "It was probably the highlight of my life," said Wyeth of the two shows. "The only bad vibes came from the outside, where everyone was freezing."

Roger Rider, a roadie for the show, was setting up the equipment and checking fuses with a cigarette dangling from his mouth. "Hey, anybody got a match?" He heard a voice behind him say, "Sure, okay." Rider saw by the light of the match that it was Chuck, and that small scene became indelibly etched in his memory. "Just like that! He said, 'Sure' and I saw that it was him!"

Rider had a prime viewpoint sitting on the edge of the stage watching both Berry and the crowd. "What really struck me was how naturally it seemed to come to him. All his movements seemed very natural, without any sign of strain . . . almost effortless." After a rousing version of "My Ding-A-Ling," the show ended when he brought 10 or so onstage

to dance to "Johnny B. Goode". "Someone took over the microphone and sang a verse," he remembers, "and it went on to the end of the night."

Rider told Berry what a great show he thought it was and Berry answered, "Glad to hear that." "Just like that!" Rider marveled. "'Glad to hear that.'"

These reactions to Berry are typical of the kind of response one gets from even the most blatant of Berry idolators. Ask one what he or she likes best about Berry, and the answer "All of it" is sure to escape their lips. Ask what part of rock & roll owes the most to Berry and the answer will most likely be the same. No more, no less.

Even into the 70s, Berry influenced the Beatles when they were on the verge of breaking up. The highlights of their last session together, reports *Shout!* author Philip Norman, were when they burst into their old Berry tunes. The first line of one of their last releases, "Come Together," is taken word for word from Berry's "You Can't Catch Me," and Jo Jo on "Get Back" is taken from Berry's "Jo Jo Gunne." There is a persistent rumor that John Lennon recorded more Berry tunes on *Rock & Roll Music* to avoid litigation.

Currently, the Berry beat seems strong as ever. The second English invasion spurred a renewed interest in primitive rockers, which seems to have hung on longer than anyone quite expected, especially in the US. The long-awaited revivals of heavy metal and folk music have instead splintered into various explorations of pop, especially funk and R & B. Also, rockabilly artists of the Bill Haley school are enjoying a new popularity, which may have started with Robert Gordon and veteran Link Wray's letter-perfect deliveries of 20-year-old material. From them came the barrage of young rockabilly enthusiasts with precariously balanced pompadours, pegged pants and string ties. Among these are the Rockats and the Stray Cats, who had a recent hit with "Runaway Boys." Those groups seemed to have a more durable style than the sneeriness of punk, which, in spite of its built-in burn-out element, still rages in some kind of Los Angeles mutation with groups like Fear, who entertain a cult group of skinheads and slam dancers in a bizarre reprise of London in 1977. As in the early days, there were movies to aid and abet each new development. Lech Kowalski's *DOA* and Penelope Gillet's *The Decline and Fall of Western Civilization* were to punk fans what *Rock Rock Rock* and *Woodstock* were to pop fans of years past.

The punk rock craze had grown out of a group of English pub-rockers who were more directly influenced by Berry. In '73, '74, and '75, bands like Dr. Feelgood, Ducks Deluxe, Kilburn and the High Roads and Mickey Jupp and Legend insistently played sweaty, ragged rock & roll when everyone else was playing disco or ballads. From these groups came Ian Dury, a Cockney songster-poet whose sense of humor, lewdness and affinity for little stories in his songs tie him directly to Berry; pure pop Nick Lowe and rockabilly retread Dave Edmonds. They in turn influenced Elvis Costello, whose album *Almost Blue*

is all country and produced by Nashville veteran Billy Sherrill.

American groups of the CBGB-Mudd club circuit like the Talking Heads and Blondie both eventually made it to the mainstream, both backed by the power of relentless rhythm sections. Interestingly, each of these groups has gone on to experiment with both very primitive Afro-tribal rhythms (as on the David Byrne-Brian Eno collaboration *My Life in the Bush of Ghosts*) and to the newest American street cult, rap and funk in the Parliament-Funkadelic mold. Debbie Harry followed up her single "Rapture" with a solo album enlisting the help of well-known funk and rap artists for *Koo-Koo*. Talking Heads, Tina Weymouth and Chris Frantz collaborated with Steven Stanley and Adrian Belew for thier infinitely listenable *Tom Tom Club*.

One of the most popular of the funk-rap scene is Rick James, king of the disco-dance clubs and whose hits reign the airwaves of any black funk station. "Give It to Me" is typical of his bawdy numbers, which he delivers with unremitting urgency while goosing the tune along with a wild array of whoops and screams. The bass line insists that you dance.

In England, however, the scene seems to bear much more emphasis on groups like Spandau Ballet, Adam and the Ants and Bow-Wow-Wow. Antmusic probably has more in common with early rave-up R & B, but the "new romantics" style often has much to do with an elaborate fashion sense, incredibly elite London dance clubs and a highly dramatic form of live presentation as the music itself. But still, there's that same sense of renegade outlaw fun (many of the costumes are take-offs of pirates and Indians) with a sort of collective, tribal gang of beat-crazy youths. Just like Bandstand.

One of the latest and most intriguing new acts to converge on the English-romantic-US-funk-rap scene is Prince, whose style show a little of each. "Controversy" is his latest single, and the line "Am I black or white/Am I gay or straight" cuts to the core of his image. With titles like "Do Me Baby" and "Head", his is a straight libidinous thrust even more explicit than Berry's. His stage gyrations are straight from Little Richard and James Brown, and his lack of guitar virtuosity alone prevents him from the potential of being a direct descendant in the Berry line of "inheritors."

But besides Berry himself, there are the Rolling Stones to contend with, who have just completed their much bally-hooed tour to universal acclamation and the epithet "The World's Greatest Rock Band." Their recent album *Tattoo You* features "Hang Five" with a distinctly Berry riff.

Berry's influence is immeasurable these days, having ricocheted off a number of translators who influenced in turn another vast array of bands whose number increases in geometric proportions.

One man who has led a lone, difficult battle to honor Berry in his home state is Jim Curtis, a professor at the University of Missouri at Colombia who teaches a course on popular culture. He has nominated Berry for an

honorary degree at the university, but he knows already the kind of trouble he's likely to encounter, since he entered Berry's name for a degree four years ago. Forty to 50 nominations are offered each year, and of these, two or three are recognized. And even at those odds, the choice for Berry would be an unusual departure from the average recipient who is typically an upstanding, respectable businessman from the community (who, it is hoped, will donate a little something to the scholarship fund) – not a black rock & roller with a prison record.

The only other degree given to a musician there was to Count Basie, another native son, in 1978. This choice fits quite well into Curtis' scheme of things, because his theory of the development of pop music states that the three great eras of pop were all started by black men from Missouri – ragtime with Scott Joplin, the big bands with Basie, and rock & roll with Chuck Berry.

Curtis, who was born in Tupelo, Mississippi, and saw Elvis Presley perform there, thinks that Elvis was obviously more important in the popularization of rock & roll, yet Berry's music may be the greater force. He remembers well listening to the daily "Maybellene" program on WHBQ from Memphis, in which the disc jockey would simply play "Maybellene" for 15 minutes straight.

"I'm something of a populist," said Curtis, "and I think this is important for us as Americans. I teach both the fine and popular arts, and I think too many people discern between them. Both of them are forms of creativity." To discount something as an art form simply because it is popular, he charges, is not a valid judgment. In an article for the *Colombia Missourian*, Curtis wrote, "Quite simply, Chuck Berry is a legend in his own time. To me, he is as much a part of Missouri's cultural heritage as Mark Twain

"Chuck Berry is undoubtedly Missouri's most famous living resident," said Curtis. "And certainly the only Missourian whose music was shot into space." After the Basie degree, the Berry degree would give the 80s "a certain completion," says Curtis. His only word from Chuck has been a note from his secretary on the ornate Berry Park stationery requesting the date of the commencement procedures. The decision is up to the Committee on Honorary Degrees and is now pending. But Curtis says if they decide against him, he'll enter Berry's name again.

In the meantime, Chuck has continued to tour and draw raves from audiences and critics alike.

In June of '79, he sat still for a short interview with Tom Zito of the *Washington Post*, and the two men hung around LaFayette Park and talked. Berry was to play the White House that night, and he'd already booked his flight back home, which would leave an hour after he came offstage. He spent the day unrecognized except by a few, and looked so anonymous that Zito said in his three-piece brown suit he looked like another "GS-9" (government employee). He reminisced a bit

with Zito about Buddy Holly and the Beatles. Along with his other loves, Berry allowed he was very fond of women. "I love those dresses with the slits in them," he told Zito. "Like that one over there at 12 o'clock." Berry started easing over toward the woman, lifting one foot over the other and nudging Zito in the process, "like Groucho Marx in pursuit of Marilyn Monroe," Zito wrote. "I bet you thought I only did the duck walk onstage," Berry said.

At a September 1980 concert in New Haven, Connecticut, Berry entertained a rather sparse crowd at the Veterans Memorial Coliseum. Writer Randall Beach noted, "The man is now 53 years old. You would think he'd be tired of playing 'Johnny B. Goode' and 'Roll Over Beethoven,' no matter how much they ignite the crowd. But just before he hit the stage, when asked if he were excited about playing the show, he said, 'I'm *forever* excited.'"

Before lining up the vocals for "My-Ding-A-Ling," Berry said, "This happens to be a sexy song. And there's nothing wrong with sex. Sex is beautiful, right? Sex is lovable, right?" "Right!" the crowd roared.

At a June 1979 concert in San Diego, during Johnny B. Goode, Berry, according to Frank Green, "hoisted a young boy up on stage, taught him to duck walk, and the two waddled across the stage twice to thunderous applause."

Robert Palmer of the *New York Times* was at the '80 gig at Heat, and only after braving the fracas at the front door was he able to catch the second show at 4 a.m., thanks to a "commando-style" full frontal assault. "It was a magnificent show," Palmer wrote. "Mr Berry sang country, calypso, and the blues; he seemed to be offering a kind of crash course in American vernacular music

In all, it was a fine night of music by an American master."

When he played the Ritz in June of '81, to a packed house, the *Times*' Stephen Holden gave him another rave review. "Mr Berry long ago stopped interpreting songs like 'Sweet Little 16' and 'School Days' from an adolescent point of view. The way he does them now, not always singing the original tunes, empasizes their pure, rhythmic momentum, which is the deepest source of their power."

If the availability of his records is any indication, Berry is again going through a resurgence of popularity. The earliest Chess recordings go for around $30 for a good recording, although some re-releases have lately surfaced for around $12. The most difficult item to find is probably the most popular of the Chess *Golden Decade* series, Volume II. Lately some French releases of that album have turned up in New York record shops, and even these are hard to find. They go for between $15 and $20 for the two-record set.

The Mercury re-releases, in general, are to be avoided: they simply don't have the zing of the Chess originals. But the *London Chuck Berry Sessions* and *Bio* on that label

are certainly worth a listen.

Since Chess was sold a few years ago, the label has been in limbo, and maybe it's because of this that Berry hasn't released anything new since 1975. The disco label Sugar Hill has most recently taken over the re-release of old Chess albums, after the material appeared on a number of independent Nashville labels.

Berry seems to have settled into a more leisurely life of performing whenever and wherever he chooses. He was seen on television most recently on a Tom Snyder interview and on a talk show for senior citizens called *Over Easy*, where he seemed relaxed and easygoing in an incongruous setting.

The revival shows go on, and most recently the Motor-town Revue was added to the list. Ben E. King, Mary Wells and even the inveterate Martha Reeves have a long way to go before comparing to the sassy Mr Berry.

In contrast to Nader's horror stories, a spokesman for New York's Ritz insisted that Berry was no problem at all in several past concerts, and they looked forward to an upcoming date.

Still, the stories about the man offstage persist. In *Jerry Lee Lewis Rocks!*, Robert Palmer finally got around to asking Lewis about the time he'd set his piano on fire before Berry was to take the stage. It was true, said Lewis. "Burned it to the ground. They forced me to do it, tellin' me I had to go on before Chuck Berry!" Lewis took a Coke bottle full of gasoline onstage, poured it over the piano with his right hand while playing the bass section with his left and ignited it while in the middle of "Great Balls of Fire." The story goes that when Lewis stalked offstage, he crowed to Berry in the wings, "I'd like to see *any* son-of-a-bitch top that!"

Then there's the Keith Richards saga. Berry had once kicked Richards off the stage when he'd jumped up to jam; Berry claimed he didn't recognize him. He once told an audience in '69 who asked if he liked the Rolling Stones, "Not to my knowledge have I talked with this person of whom you spoke Dick Jagger?"

At his Ritz concert in '81, Richards was spied in Berry's dressing room along with a number of fans. When Berry left, Richards tossed off an unintelligible comment after him and Berry dove back in the room, swinging. After Ritz security staff separated them, Berry stormed off.

For over a dozen years, Berry's been talking about the book he's going to release, based on a journal he's kept since 1956. The last report on it had it due for publication in February 1980, but it has yet to materialize. It is his standard response to requests for interviews that since he's so often been misconstrued in the past, he's going to wait and publish his own tell-all version. The book will undoubtedly be one of the great documents of rock & roll if it is ever released. The talent he's toured with alone could fill volumes.

But still he tours and plays, displaying the same magic that has enthralled fans for years. He has his off days, sometimes looking like his heart's not really in the performance and maybe relying on his Maybellene-School

Days-Johnny B. Goode medley so much that it all begins to sound alike. But at a concert like the one at the Ritz, when Berry meets the kids, the ones who came to dance, he's irresistible and an ever self-renewing national resource. Seeing him live makes the difference. If you're over 25, you feel old and young at the same time. You wish you were like those teenagers, hearing this stuff for the first time, but then the music itself is at once so full of memory and rejuvenation that you feel sorry that the ones younger than "Maybellene" have missed out on so much.

There is something almost shaman-esque about him, and his talisman is the guitar. Standing there with the frets up close to his face, fingering effortlessly and looking earnestly out at the crowd, he is a paterfamilia of the first order. Lest he be mistaken for some kind of mystical seeker, look at the images he conjures: burger sizzling on a grill, a car radio blaring, the top down on a summer night, a carhop on roller skates, a sixteen-year-old girl who understands what the old men never will, the school bell at 3:00, a jukebox that plays two hits for a dime, a phone booth, the expanse of a country of little and big towns linked by a long, long open road.

"Humor with an underlying sadness,' Tom Zito wrote of his music. "Not so much black as American; not so much a mirror of adolescence as timelessness."

Promoter Richard Nader spent a good deal of time in an interview detailing the trouble Berry had put him through, and the frustration he'd felt knowing him for a dozen years and never really gaining his trust. At one point, he brought up the line Berry says to the actor portraying Alan Freed in *American Hot Wax*: "I'll do it for rock & roll," meaning he'd perform free. "I laughed when I heard that line," said Nader. "He fuckin' *raped* rock & roll."

At the end of the interview, however, Nader paused and mused on the man's history, both the music and his infuriating habits. "In the end," he said, "I think it will all be unwritten."

Singles		
Maybellene/ Wee Wee Hours	*Chess 1604*	5/55
Thirty Days/ Together (We Will Always Be)	*Chess 1610*	/55
No Money Down/ The Downbound Train	*Chess 1615*	/56
Drifting Heart/ Roll Over Beethoven	*Chess 1626*	5/56
Too Much Monkey Business/ Roll Over Beethoven	*Chess 1635*	/56
You Can't Catch Me/ Havana Moon	*Chess 1645*	/56
School Days/ Deep Feeling	*Chess 1653*	2/57
Oh Baby Doll/ La Juanda	*Chess 1664*	6/57
Rock & Roll Music/ Blue Feeling	*Chess 1671*	/57
Sweet Little Sixteen/ Reelin' and Rockin'	*Chess 1683*	1/58
Johnny B. Goode/ Around and Around	*Chess 1691*	3/58
Beautiful Delilah/ Vacation Time	*Chess 1697*	6/58
Carol/ Hey Pedro	*Chess 1700*	8/58
Sweet Little Rock & Roller/ Jo Jo Gunne	*Chess 1709*	11/58
Merry Christmas Baby/ Run Rudolph Run	*Chess 1714*	11/58
Anthony Boy/ That's My Desire	*Chess 1716*	1/59
Almost Grown/ Little Queenie	*Chess 1722*	3/59
Memphis, Tennessee/ Back in the USA	*Chess 1729*	6/59

Broken Arrow/ My Childhood Sweetheart	*Chess 1737*	9/59
Let It Rock (Rocking on the Rail Road)/ Too Pooped to Pop	*Chess 1747*	3/60
Bye Bye Johnny/ Worried Life Blues	*Chess 1754*	6/60
I Got to Find My Baby/ Mad Lad	*Chess 1763*	9/60
Jaguar and Thunderbird/ Our Little Rendezvous	*Chess 1767*	12/60
I'm Talking About You/ Little Star	*Chess 1779*	3/61
Come On/ Go Go Go	*Chess 1799*	12/61
Diploma for Two/ I'm Talkin' About You	*Chess 1853*	7/63
Memphis/ Sweet Little 16 (Surfin' USA)	*Chess 1866*	9/63
Nadine/ O Rangutang	*Chess 1883*	3/64
No Particular Place to Go/ You Too	*Chess 1898*	6/64
Brenda Lee/ You Never Can Tell	*Chess 1906*	9/64
Bo's Beat/ Chuck's Beat	*Checker 1089*	9/64
Go Bobby Soxer/ Little Marie	*Chess 1912*	12/64
Promised Land/ Things I Used to Do	*Chess 1916*	12/64
Dear Dad/ Lonely School Days	*Chess 1926*	6/65
Lonely School Days/ Ramona Say Yes	*Chess 1963*	6/66
Club Nitty Gritty/	*Mercury*	

Laugh and Cry	*72643*	12/66
Back to Memphis/ **I Do Really Love You**	*Mercury* *72680*	6/67
Feelin' It/ **It Hurts Me Too**	*Mercury* *72748*	12/67
Louie to Frisco/ **Ma Dear**	*Mercury* *72840*	9/68
Good Looking Woman/ **It's Too Dark in There**	*Mercury* *72963*	12/69
Have Mercy Judge/ **Tulane**	*Chess 2090*	6/70
Johnny B. Goode/ **My Ding A Ling**	*Chess 2131*	9/72
Let's Boogie/ **Reelin' and Rockin'**	*Chess 2136*	12/72
Bio/ **Roll 'Em Pete**	*Chess 2140*	12/73
Nadine/ **Roll Over Beethoven**	*Chess 9010*	12/73
Maybellene/ **Rock & Roll Music**	*Chess 9020*	12/73
Johnny B. Goode/ **Sweet Little 16**	*Chess 9021*	12/73
Memphis/ **School Days**	*Chess 9030*	12/73
Oh What A Thrill/	*Atco 7203*	/75

There are scores of other "re-releases" including: Carol/Johnny B. Goode (ERC 224); My Ding a Ling (ERC 227); Memphis/Rock & Roll Music (ERC 226, Mercury 30146); Maybellene/Roll Over Beethoven (ERC 227; Mercury 30143).

EPs

Brown-Eyed Handsome Man/ Too Much Monkey Business/ Deep Feeling/ School Day	*Chess 5118*	/57
La Juanda/ Blue Feeling/ Rock & Roll Music/ Oh Baby Doll	*Chess 5119*	/57
Sweet Little 16/ Rockin' at the Philharmonic/ Guitar Boogie/ Reelin' and Rockin'	*Chess 5121*	/58
Beautiful Delilah/ Vacation Time/ Carol/ Hey Pedro	*Chess 5124*	/58
Johnny B. Goode/ Around and Around/ Jo Jo Gunne/ Sweet Little Rock & Roller	*Chess 5126*	/58

AFTER SCHOOL SESSION *Chess 1426* 10/58
School Days; Wee Wee Hours; Brown-Eyed Handsome Man; Too Much Monkey Business; Deep Feeling; Rolli Polli; Berry Pickin'; Together; No Money Down; Havana Moon; Downbound Train; Drifting Heart.

ONE DOZEN BERRYS *Chess 1432* 10/58
Sweet Little 16; Rock & Roll Music; Blue Ceiling; Rockin' at the Philharmonic; Juanda Espanol; Oh Baby Doll; Guitar Boogie; In- Go; Low Ceiling; How You've Changed; It Don't Take But a Few Minutes.

CHUCK BERRY IS ON TOP *Chess 1435* 9/59
Almost Grown; Carol; Maybellene; Johnny B. Goode; Little Queenie; Anthony Boy; Sweet Little Rock & Roller; Jo Jo Gunne; Around and Around; Roll Over Beethoven; Hey Pedro; Blues for Hawaiians.

ROCKIN' AT THE HOPS *Chess 1448* 6/60
Bye Bye Johnny; Worried Life Blues; Down the Road a Piece; Confessin' the Blues; Too Pooped to Pop; Mad Lad; I Got to Find My Baby; Betty Jean; Childhood Sweetheart; Broken Arrow; Driftin' the Blues; Let it Rock.

NEW JUKE BOX HITS *Chess 1456* 6/61
I'm Talkin' About You; Diploma for Two; Rip It Up; Thirteen Questions Method; Way It was Before; Away With You; Don't You Lie to Me; Little Star; Route 66; Sweet Sixteen; Stop and Listen; Run Around.

TWIST *Chess 1465* 6/62

Maybellene; Roll Over Beethoven; Oh Baby Doll; Round and Round; Come On; Let It Rock; Reelin' and Rockin'; School Days; Almost Grown; Sweet Little 16; Thirty Days; Johnny B. Goode; Rock & Roll Music; Back in the USA. (Later issued under the title MORE CHUCK BERRY (Chess 1465)).

CHUCK BERRY ON STAGE *Chess 1480* 7/63

Memphis; Sweet Little 16; Rockin' on the Railroad; Maybellene; Surfing Stella; Go Go Go; Brown-Eyed Handsome Man; Still Got the Blues; Jaguar and the Thunderbirds; I Just Want to Make Love to You; All Aboard; The Man and the Donkey; Trick or Treat.

CHUCK BERRY'S GREATEST HITS *Chess 1485* 6/64

Roll Over Beethoven; Rock & Roll Music; Too Much Monkey Business; Oh Baby Doll; Johnny B. Goode; Nadine; Thirty Days; Memphis; Maybellene; Sweet Little 16; Brown-Eyed Handsome Man.

TWO GREAT GUITARS (With Bo Diddley) *Checker 2991* 9/64

Liverpool Drive; Chuck's Beat; Bo's Beat; When the Saints Go Marching In.

ST LOUIS TO LIVERPOOL *Chess 1488* 12/64
Little Marie; You Never Can Tell; Bobby Soxer; No Particular Place to Go; Merry Christmas Baby; Our Little Rendezvous; You Two; Night Beat; Promised Land; Things I Used to Do; Liverpool Beat; Brenda Lee. (Some issues contain a version of "How Great Thou Art" instead of "Brenda Lee.")

CHUCK BERRY IN LONDON *Chess 1495* 7/65
My Little Love-Lights; She Once Was Mine; After It's Over; I Got a Booking; You Came a Long Way from St. Louis; Night Beat; St. Louis Blues; His Daughter Caroline; Dear Dad; Jamaica Farewell; Butterscotch; Song of My Love; Why Should We End This Way; I Want to be Your Driver.

FRESH BERRYS *Chess 1498* 10/65
It Wasn't Me; Run Joe; Every Day We Rock & Roll; One for My Baby; Welcome Back, Pretty Baby; It's My Own Business; Right off Rampart Street; Vaya Con Dios; Merrily We Rock & Roll; My Mustang Ford; Ain't That Just Like a Woman; Wee Hour Blues.

GOLDEN HITS *Mercury 21103*
(stereo) 61103 3/67
Sweet Little 16; Memphis; Back in the USA; School Days; Maybellene; Johnny B. Goode; Rock & Roll Music; Thirty Days; Carol; Club Nitty Gritty; Roll Over Beethoven.

CHUCK BERRY'S GOLDEN DECADE (reissue) — *Chess 1514* 3/67; *60023* /72

Maybellene; Deep Feeling; Johnny B. Goode; Wee Wee Hours; Nadine; Thirty Days; Brown-Eyed Handsome Man; Roll Over Beethoven; No Particular Place to Go; Havana Moon; Memphis; School Days; Almost Grown; Too Much Monkey Business; Oh Baby Doll; Reelin' & Rockin'; You Can't Catch Me; Too Pooped to Pop; Bye Bye Johnny; Round and Round; Sweet Little 16; Rock & Roll Music; Back in the USA; Anthony Boy.

CHUCK BERRY IN MEMPHIS — *Mercury 21123*; *(stereo) 61123* 9/67

Back to Memphis; I Do Really Love You; My Heart Will Always Belong to You; Ramblin' Rose; Sweet Little Rock & Roller; Oh Baby Doll; Check Me Out; It Hurts Me Too; Bring Another Drink; So Long, Goodnight, Well It's Time to Go.

SWEET LITTLE ROCK & ROLLER — *Pickwick 3345* /67

(previously on Mercury)

Sweet Little Rock & Roller; Oh Baby Doll; C.C. Rider; Check Me Out; Carol; Back to Memphis; Bring Another Drink; It Hurts Me Too; So Long, Goodnight, Well It's Time to Go.

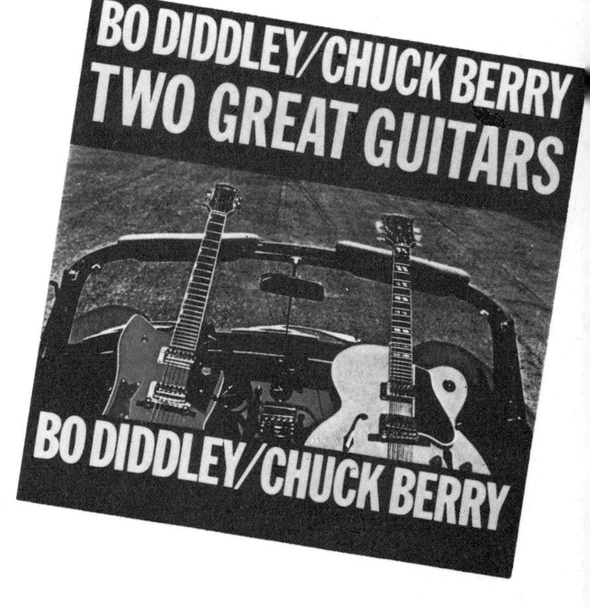

FILLMORE AUDITORIUM *Mercury 21138 (stereo) 61138* 9/67

Driftin' Blues; Hootchie Cootchie Blues; Johnny B. Goode; See See Rider; Feelin' It; Flying Home; It Hurts Me Too; Fillmore Blues; Wee Baby Blues; Medley.

FROM ST. LOUIE TO FRISCO *Mercury 61176* 11/68

Louie to Frisco; Ma Dear; The Love I Lost; I Love Her, I Love Her; Little Fox; Rock Cradle Rock; Soul Rockin'; I Can't Believe; Misery; My Tambourine; Oh Captain; Mum's the Word.

CONCERTO IN B. GOODE *Mercury 61223* 6/69

Good Looking Woman; My Woman; It's Too Dark in There; Put Her Down; Concerto in B. Goode.

ROCK, ROCK, ROCK & ROLL *Mercury 6463044* /69

Maybellene; Back in the USA: Johnny B. Goode; Rock & Roll Music; Carol; Sweet Little 16; Roll Over Beethoven; Let it Rock; Sweet Little Rock & Roller; Oh Baby Doll; So Long, Goodnight, Well It's Time to Go.

BACK HOME *Chess 1550* 9/70

Tulane; Have Mercy Judge; Gun; I'm a Rocker; Flyin' Home; Fish and Chips; Some People.

THE LONDON CHUCK BERRY SESSIONS *Chess 60020* 5/72
Let's Boogie; Mean Old World; My Ding a Ling; I Will Not Let You Go; London Berry Blues; I Love You; Reelin' and Rockin'; Johnny B. Goode.

SAN FRANCISCO DUES *Chess 50008* /72
Lonely School Days; My Dream; Bordeaux in my Pirough (others not reported).

ST LOUIS TO FRISCO TO MEMPHIS *Mercury SRM-2 6501* 10/72
Rockin' at the Fillmore; Every Day I Have the Blues; See See Rider; Driftin' Blues; Feelin' It; Flying Home; I'm Your Hoochie Coochie Man; It Hurts Me Too; Fillmore Blues; Wee Baby Blues; Johnny B. Goode; Louie to Frisco; Ma Dear, Ma Dear; Soul Rockin'; Check Me Out; Little Fox; Back to Memphis; Misery; My Tambourine; It's Too Dark in There; I Do Really Love You; I Can't Believe; My Heart Will Always Belong to You; So Long, Goodnight, Well It's Time to Go.

BIO
(with Elephant's Memory) *Chess 50043* 9/73
Hello Little Girl, Goodbye; Woodpecker; Rain Eyes; Aimlessly Driftin'; Got It and Gone; Talkin' About My Buddy.

GOLDEN DECADE (Vol. 2) *Chess 60023* 3/73
Carol; You Never Can Tell; No Money Down; Together We Will Always Be; Mad Lad; Run Rudolph Run; Let It Rock; Sweet Little Rock and Roller; It Don't Take But a Few Minutes; I'm Talking About You; Driftin' Blues; Go Go Go; Jaguar and the Thunderbird; Little Queenie; Betty Jean; Guitar Boogie; Down the Road Apiece; Merry Christmas Baby; The Promised Land; Jo Jo Gunne; Don't You Lie to Me; Rockin' at the Philharmonic; La Juanda; Come On.

GOLDEN DECADE (Vol. 3) *Chess 60028* /74
Beautiful Delilah; Go Bobby Soxer; I Got to Find My Baby; Worried Life Blues; Rolli Polli; Downbound Train; Broken Arrow; Confessin' the Blues; Driftin' Heart; Ingo; The Man and the Donkey; St. Louis Blues; Our Little Rendezvous; Childhood Sweetheart; Blues for Hawaiians; Hey Pedro; My Little Lovelight; Little Marie; County Line; Viva, Viva Rock & Roll; House of Blue Lights; Time Was; Blue on Blue; Oh Yeah.

CHUCK BERRY '75 *Chess 60032* 3/75
Swanee River; I'm Just a Name; I Just Want to Make Love to You; Too Late; South of the Border; Hi-Heel Sneakers; You Are My Sunshine; My Baby; Baby What You Want Me to Do; A Deuce; Shake Rattle and Roll; Sue Answer; Don't You Lie to Me.

ROCK IT *Atco 38-118* /79

Move It; Oh What a Thrill; I Need You Baby; If I Were; House Lights; I Never Thought; Havana Moon; Wuden't Me; California; Pass Away.

More "re-releases":

CHUCK BERRY:ALL TIME ROCK & ROLL PARTY HITS	*6310-130*	1/75
ST LOUIS TO FRISCO TO MEMPHIS	*Phillips 6619.008*	3/75
SIX TWO FIVE	*Driving Wheel 1001*	3/77
MOTORVATIN'	*Chess 9286*	5/77
GREATEST HITS (differs slightly from Chess version – Archive of Folk and Jazz	*Everest Records 321*	3/77
THE BEST OF THE BEST OF CHUCK BERRY	*Gusto 004*	/78
CHUCK BERRY: MR. ROCK & ROLL	*on French VIP label*	/81
CHUCK BERRY LIVE	*Magnum SSS-36*	/81

Compilations on which Berry has a cut or more:

Title	Label	Date
AMERICAN GRAFFITI (Soundtrack)	*MCA 2-8001*	/73
AMERICAN HOT WAX (Soundtrack)	*A&M 6500*	/79
CHUCK BERRY AND HIS FRIENDS	*Aristocrat/ Brookville 1274*	/74
THE BLUES (Vols. 1 & 2)	*Argo 4026 4027*	9/63
HEAVY HEADS VOYAGE 2 (Muddy Waters, Little Walter, Chuck Berry and others)	*Chess 1528*	3/69
HOUND DOG'S ORIGINAL ROCK & ROLL MEMORY TIME	*Atlantic 9068*	12/62
MURRAY THE K'S BLASTS FROM THE PAST	*Chess 1461*	12/61
OLDIES BUT GOODIES (Vols. 10 11 and 12)	*OSR8860, 61, 62*	
REMEMBER HOW GREAT (Vol. 1)	*Roulette 42027*	9/69
RHYTHM & BLUES CHRISTMAS	*United Artists LW-654*	
SUPER OLDIES (Vols. 1 and 6)	*Capitol T-2562 STBB-401*	
TREASURE TUNES FROM THE VAULT	*Chess 1474*	12/62